» **praise for** *momentum*

"Digital, mobile, these aren't things, they're lifestyles. Businesses now compete in an era of digital Darwinism. We know how evolution works. You thrive or you don't. Shama will help you understand not only what's different, but what to do about it, and how to get better results."

—Brian Solis, Brian Solis, leading digital analyst, futurist, author of *X: The Experience When Business Meets Design*

"*Momentum* provides important insights concerning the seismic shift that has permanently transformed marketing and branding. Shama understands the complexities of consumer behavior in our new, social media-driven, global economy, and offers concrete principles that will drive success for any business or organization. With *Momentum*, any business leader can learn to artfully transition a traditional marketing strategy into an agile, integrated and customer-focused operation that draws in and engages consumers."

—Gloria Larson, President at Bentley University

"In a market where disruption is the norm, even the smartest leaders are unsure how to adjust their marketing plan to meet tomorrow's demands. Momentum shows you how to create a sustainable plan that allows you to attract more customers and profits, no matter what may come your way."

—Charlene Li, author of *The Engaged Leader* **and** *Open Leadership,* **coauthor of** *Groundswell,* **and principal analyst at Altimeter, a Prophet Company**

"Without *Momentum*, building a business is one big uphill climb—with it, it's one sweet ride!"

—John Jantsch, author of *Duct Tape Marketing* **and** *The Referral Engine*

"Today's marketers and business leaders need to learn how to get in sync with their customers and anticipate their constantly shifting needs. That's a challenging task, but reading *Momentum* will speed you through the learning curve."

—Tom Davis, CMO of Forbes Media

"In the fast-moving world of digital strategy, Shama Hyder stands out as a true expert. In *Momentum*, she shares smart, actionable, hype-free strategies to help your brand break through. If you want to harness the true power of marketing in the digital age for your business, read this book."

—Dorie Clark, author of *Stand Out* and *Reinventing You* and adjunct professor at Duke University's Fuqua School of Business

"Want to build a likeable brand that attracts customers and stands out? If so, you need *Momentum*. Actionable and easy to digest, this book helps you unlock the code for marketing success in the Digital Age."

—Dave Kerpen, *New York Times* bestselling author of *Likeable Social Media*

"Timely and on target, *Momentum* shows you precisely how to use today's modern marketing to outflank your competition. Great examples throughout and highly recommended!"

—Jay Baer, president of Convince & Convert and *New York Times* bestselling author of *Youtility*

"*Momentum* offers a blueprint for transformation that can help any marketer flourish in the digital world. This is the best marketing book I've read in years."

—Charles Marsh, Oscar Stauffer Professor of Journalism and Mass Communications at the University of Kansas

momentum

How to **Propel** Your
Marketing and **Transform** Your
Brand in the Digital Age

momentum

Shama Hyder

BenBella Books, Inc.
Dallas, Texas

BenBella Books, Inc.
PO Box 572028
Dallas, TX 75357-2028
www.benbellabooks.com
Send feedback to feedback@benbellabooks.com

Printed in the United States of America
10   9   8   7   6   5   4   3   2   1
978-1-942952-25-1 (hardcover)
978-1-942952-26-8 (electronic)

Library of Congress Cataloging-in-Publication Data available upon request.
LCCN: 2015043230

Editing by Leah Wilson
Copyediting by Shannon Kelly
Proofreading by Cape Cod
    Compositors, Inc. and Brittney
    Martinez
Text design by Publishers' Design and
    Production Services, Inc.
Jacket design by Sarah Dombrowsky

Indexing by Amy Murphy Indexing &
    Editorial
Text composition by PerfecType,
    Nashville, TN
Front cover design by Faceout Studio,
    Emily Weigel
Printed by Lake Book Manufacturing

Distributed by Perseus Distribution
www.perseusdistribution.com

To place orders through Perseus Distribution:
Tel: (800) 343-4499
Fax: (800) 351-5073
E-mail: orderentry@perseusbooks.com

Special discounts for bulk sales (minimum of 25 copies) are available. Please contact Aida Herrera at aida@benbellabooks.com.

To the entire team at The Marketing Zen Group,
for their passion and hard work

To our clients, who make it all possible
with their belief in us and support

And to you, dear reader, for your precious time
and attention

contents

chapter 1

The New Ecosystem:
Building Momentum

M OMENTUM.

It's the thrill of a roller coaster gaining speed.

It's an unstoppable train barreling down the tracks.

And it's what every marketer wants in a campaign.

Whether it's a video going viral or a blog post going from one share to thousands in just a few days, when a marketing initiative has real momentum, it is nothing short of pure magic.

And just like magic, it seems impossible to re-create, impossible to develop using a strategic, systematic approach.

But I'm here to let you in on the magician's secret: You can achieve that momentum yourself by following five simple principles—principles that will allow you to consistently deliver great results with your marketing.

Today, the digital landscape is constantly changing, and news travels at the speed of a tweet. But there is a way to cut through the noise and build that momentum for your own campaigns.

Want to know the secret?

First, let me ask you this.

What does digital marketing mean to you?

Posting on Facebook and Twitter a few times a week? Emailing a list of subscribers? Cranking out blog posts every few days? Tweaking your website to make it mobile responsive? Trying out the latest new social media platforms to find the trendiest ways of connecting with your audience?

Has digital marketing just added more items to your to-do list?

It doesn't have to be this way. Effective digital marketing isn't about embracing every new tool available to today's marketer— it's about turning your entire approach to marketing on its head.

» The Future Has Arrived

Imagine you're going for a jog. You've got your trusty fitness band on, to help you keep track of all the miles you're running and all the calories you're burning. Maybe it'll automatically post your route to Facebook in case your friends want to join you. Or maybe you can even tap it to your friends' bands to compare data and start a little friendly competition.

Now imagine that you're almost at the end of your jogging route, when suddenly, your fitness band shows you an offer for a free sports drink at a store nearby. All you have to do to redeem it is tap the link on your band at checkout. You're hot, tired, and thirsty, and the drink is right there. It's a no-brainer, right?

Next, another offer might pop up, encouraging you to share that same link—along with a picture of yourself, post-jog, sweaty and smiling with that sports drink—to your Facebook page; the link would provide a free drink to any of your Facebook friends who clicked on it. You're not one to keep a good deal to yourself, or to miss out on a great opportunity to share, so of course you post the link and pic. "So happy my little 5-mile morning jog can help get my friends a free drink, too!" Score!

If you're a jogger, you might think of this as an incredibly convenient way to rehydrate on the cheap right when you need it most and feel some serious appreciation toward the sports drink company for being so thoughtful and generous.

If you're a marketer, you see this as the exciting new reality of building marketing momentum in the digital age.

Instead of blindly sticking millions of identical coupons in newspapers and mailers, hoping that a small percentage of them might land in the right hands and evoke a response, marketers can now target customers individually, at the time, in the place, and through the medium that will make them most likely to respond.

This is nothing less than a *seismic shift*.

The ability to tailor marketing not just to a certain region or a specific demographic, but to an individual—and not just to an individual, but to that individual in the optimal place, time, and way—has revolutionized the nature of marketing.

It's not just the medium that's changed here. It's not even just the ability to customize marketing messages to individual customers. It's the entire mindset behind marketing. The entire approach.

And this new approach is centered around the creation of real momentum in your marketing: meaningful momentum that helps you reach your goals.

Let's take a closer look at how we got here.

» A History of Push Marketing

Marketing is not a new concept. If you've got something to sell, you've got to tell people about it, or no one will ever buy. And since competition isn't new, either, you've also got to explain why customers should choose your product or service over everyone else's.

Ancient marketplaces teemed with merchants crying their wares, each trying to outdo the others. Latin graffiti has even been found scrawled on a wall in Pompeii, advertising the fish sauce the doomed town was famous for: "Scaurus's best garum, mackerel-based, from Scaurus's manufacturers."

When the printing press came onto the scene, print marketing was suddenly possible. Ads like the following from 1771 appeared in early American newspapers: "James Gardner, Carpenter and Joiner, begs Leave to inform the Publick that he has opened Shop behind the Church. All Gentlemen who please to favour him with their Orders may depend upon his Punctuality, and their Business being well executed. N.B. He makes Window Sashes, on reasonable Terms."

As time went on, the advent of radio, and later TV, meant that marketing took on new layers of sophistication. Still, the approach remained the same: a business pushing its message out to people, hoping that message was appealing enough to compel them to buy.

There were definitely benefits to marketing as it existed by the late twentieth century. Businesses had complete control over their messaging—over the way they and their product were presented. Thanks to mass media's mass audiences, they could reach large groups of people with a single ad. Marketing collateral could be put together quickly, because looking for customer input wasn't a step in its development. And because of this freedom to create elaborate marketing campaigns without customer feedback affecting their direction, creative marketing really could—and often did—ascend to the status of art.

But when the internet went mainstream in the 1990s, all that began to change.

Suddenly, people had choices as to the marketing material they consumed. The information they had access to wasn't limited to what they saw in the commercials that companies decided to push at them or to what they read in ads in magazines or newspapers or on billboards—they could now take the initiative themselves to go online and research that company, its products or services, and its reputation. As an audience, they were now divided into smaller segments; they were no longer watching the same show on TV as everyone else at the same time as everyone else, or reading the same paper as everyone else each day. Cable and home video recording, and later new technology like DVRs and streaming video, allowed consumers to watch whatever they wanted, whenever they wanted. Countless different websites provided information tailored to specific interests 24/7. Instead of being advertised to whether they liked it or not, customers now gained the ability to opt in to marketing, supplying their email addresses directly to companies because they wanted to see their messages. The consumer was now in control; the company, not so much.

Faced with this sudden transformation in customer behavior and expectations, marketers found their old methods just weren't working as well anymore. Audiences that were now accustomed to choosing which ads they received came to see the old model of marketing as intrusive, pushy, and irrelevant to their unique interests.

» The Advent of Pull Marketing

In order to tailor their methods to fit this new trend, marketers developed pull marketing, an approach that harnesses the power of internet search engines and social media to draw people in to your site rather than to a competitors'.

Before the internet, potential customers had limited resources for deciding which business to purchase a product from. Ads created by the company and in-person visits or phone calls with salespeople were the only ways to learn more about that company's offerings—and that content, which was "pushed" at the consumer, was all tightly controlled by the company itself.

Now, however, prospective customers were free to research companies and products on their own. One way they did this was via search engines—neutral third parties where a customer might end up reading the company's page, or its competitor's, or even a review site. Or consumers could find out what peers thought of certain companies or products through social media, which was (and is) even harder for companies to influence than a search engine: A friend might share an experience they'd had with a business, post a link to a blog post reviewing a product, or even just "like" a company's post or page.

Given these new ways in which consumers were finding information, companies needed to draw customers in rather than disseminate information out; they needed to make sure the company was appearing as a top choice in online searches for the types of products or services they offered. They needed to employ pull marketing.

So how did marketers accomplish this? By learning more about their customers and target audiences. Research into the phrases people actually used to search for their products online led to ever more effective ways of funneling high-quality search engine traffic to their sites. Engagement with people on social media led to clearer insight into what interested their particular audience. By looking at which posts garnered clicks, likes, and comments, marketers could fine-tune their approach. Creating content based on that information gave companies the tools to more effectively attract traffic to *their* site, where they could then send the brand message they wanted to convey to consumers, versus contending with the various messages consumers might receive elsewhere.

Pull marketing basically put consumers in charge of marketing. They had the power to customize the way they wanted to be marketed to, and they wanted to be marketed to only by the companies they had invited to do so, using the medium they preferred. There was no going back. Successful marketers had to embrace this new normal and cater to this new consumer expectation of control.

One example is permission-based marketing. In its earliest days, email was still considered a venue for push marketing by many companies. Companies could buy lists of email addresses online and blast out their message to thousands of recipients who might never have heard of them before. Today those sales emails would be classified as spam. The flood of unsolicited emails eventually became such a problem that Congress took action, making unsolicited mass emails illegal. Asking website visitors to opt in to marketing emails was marketers' response to the crackdown.

The benefits to pull marketing are clear. By engaging *with* the audience in a two-way, personalized conversation, rather than talking *to* them with a one-way, generic ad, companies can deliver their message in the most effective way possible—and by taking an active role in marketing, consumers get the information they actually want and need. This two-way conversation also means companies are able to take consumer responses into consideration when planning future campaigns, making their campaigns more and more effective. All the data companies gather from engaging the consumer makes it possible to target customers more specifically.

The key difference between the two approaches? Push marketing is all about the company. Pull marketing is all about the consumer.

» Beyond Push and Pull: An Integrated Ecosystem

So what's the problem here? Why isn't every company happily pursuing their inbound, pull marketing plans in this new digital landscape and reaping success after success?

Because of the difficulty of engaging today's segmented audience.

This is not your mother's internet. It's not just a matter of websites and email anymore. Social media is a huge and vital but constantly changing force in pull marketing—and like your audience, it's just about as segmented as you can get. There's Facebook and Twitter, Instagram and Pinterest and everything in between—different social media platforms preferred by people with different interests from different demographics. When companies decide to make the shift from outbound, push marketing to inbound, pull marketing, they are often at a loss as to which platforms to use.

Beyond that, many companies struggle with integrating their digital marketing efforts with their traditional ones. Isn't it too risky, they wonder, to scrap their old marketing tactics completely, and revamp their entire approach? So instead, they just add in bits and pieces of digital where they think it might fit into their traditional strategy, or even keep the two separate, so that a misstep in one arena doesn't affect the other.

That's not to say you should blindly jump into new marketing options—become active in a new channel or execute some new "best practice" tactic for the sake of staying current, only to exhaust yourself without any results to show for it. That's an easy way to find your entire marketing program losing its focus.

Instead, the answer is to take a strategic approach to all the new opportunities out there: new social media platforms; new ways your prospects are willing to engage with you; new ways you can get your marketing messages out via your website, email marketing program, and more.

There is a way to keep pace with the rapidly evolving marketing world, see continuing positive results, and most important, do so while keeping your sanity.

The game of marketing is no longer about which digital marketing tool is the most effective. It's not even just about push versus pull anymore. We are operating in an entirely new ecosystem, a digital paradigm in which ever-changing digital tools play a key role, but are not the sole drivers of success. While the novelty of the new marketing tools at our disposal can be captivating, it is important to remember the real goal: using those tools strategically, in a way that builds marketing momentum.

There are a number of key differences between the old model of marketing and the new ecosystem:

Old Paradigm: **Fixed marketing**
New Paradigm: **Agile marketing**
In the old model of marketing, campaigns were developed and then executed as planned, no matter what the response was during their run. Now, real-time analytics tracking during campaigns allows marketers to turn on a dime and shift gears instantly to avoid disaster or take advantage of new insights or opportunities.

Old Paradigm: **Brand-led**
New Paradigm: **Customer-driven**
Marketing messages used to be based on what a company wanted to convey about itself. Now they're based on what a product or service allows customers to convey to others about themselves. And not only that—a modern marketer's entire strategy is based on the information he gathers about his audience and is customized to fit their preferences.

Old Paradigm: **Focuses on push versus pull marketing**
New Paradigm: **Integrates all marketing channels**
Where once marketers would choose between various distinct options—outbound versus inbound, traditional versus digital—now, companies are strategically integrating their marketing methods and channels. Marketers have realized that integration yields a much higher ROI than any single method or medium could ever hope to.

Old Paradigm: **Quantity dictates strategies**
New Paradigm: **Quality dictates strategies**
In the old marketing paradigm, frequency of posting was the key to success; quality was secondary. Now, quality is the guiding principle for content, and determines its success in search and social media, as well as with its readers.

Old Paradigm: **Branches out to whatever is new**
New Paradigm: **Utilizes relationships to grow**

While it used to be common for businesses to jump on the bandwagon and try every new platform that gained some popularity, novelty does not equal effectiveness, and spreading marketing efforts too thin is never a good idea. Now, smart marketers understand that instead of branching out, looking within can be the key to success. Some of the most effective digital marketing strategies can come from collaboration and integration with partners, customers, and vendors.

Old Paradigm: **Forces old metrics on new platforms**
New Paradigm: **Successfully decodes digital data points**

Just as the marketing ecosystem has changed, so have the data points that determine success in the digital arena, and trying to force old push marketing metrics onto these new platforms is just setting yourself up for failure. Understanding how these new digital metrics affect overall goals is a vital part of the new model of marketing.

Old Paradigm: **Uses digital marketing**
New Paradigm: **Embraces digital mindset**

Using digital marketing means including digital marketing activities as part of a marketing strategy. Embracing a digital mindset means rethinking your entire approach to marketing. Doing so can mean major change—but it's the only way to find success in this new ecosystem.

The old marketing model focused on choosing and pursuing just one marketing methodology—traditional or digital, inbound or outbound, push or pull. But in today's world, where the line between the two is quickly blurring, that forced choice is one that no longer makes sense. Marketers embracing the new ecosystem recognize that, rather than choosing between options, we have to integrate them strategically.

Take event marketing, a very traditional marketing method. You invite prospects and customers to your event and hand them swag bags full of marketing messaging—a very "push" approach. But today, throughout the event, those attendees are also active on social media, using your event hashtag on Twitter and other platforms, interacting with other attendees and hopefully your marketing team—a very "pull" approach, as it relies on the willingness of those customers to engage with your message online.

Your traditional event marketing channel also is no longer limited to just reaching attendees. Simply by collecting some materials from presenters and setting up cameras, you can now have a virtual, digital audience that is downloading speakers' slide decks, watching live streams of event presentations, and engaging with attendees via social media in real time. What was once a marketing campaign restricted to a single physical space is now a marketing campaign that is global.

Some companies are even taking event marketing completely digital. SafetyLine is a Canadian SaaS, or Software as a Service, that offers a safety monitoring solution for people who work alone. It ran a campaign in which it threw an online "launch party" for its new website. The digital event mimicked a more traditional in-person event, with presentations in the form of webinars, and even provided attendees with "virtual swag bags" with coupons and e-book downloads.

One caveat in this new ecosystem is making sure you aren't running a campaign just *because* it's new or different, but rather because that campaign is the best way to meet the particular goal at hand. In SafetyLine's case, a fully digital event marketing effort made *more* sense than a physical event, because the main goal of the campaign was to get its email subscriber list to reconnect with the company and take the steps necessary for SafetyLine to become compliant with Canada's new anti-spam law. It just happened that the team decided a fun new marketing tactic would be the best way to achieve that goal.

Organizations that follow the old paradigm of marketing let tools dictate their campaigns and strategies. Often, they ask, "What can we do with this new tool?" when they should be asking, "Can this new tool help us with our existing business goals and strategies?"

SafetyLine's marketing team realized that a new tool—the ability to host a virtual event marketing campaign with elements that approximated an in-person event—could help it achieve a very specific goal. Voilá! Integrated, strategic digital marketing—a poster child for marketing in the new ecosystem.

» How Your Company Can Embrace the New Ecosystem, Too

In this book, I'll be introducing the five essential principles to building marketing momentum in the digital age: agility, customer focus, integration, content curation, and cross-pollination.

Here's what to expect from each chapter:

Chapter 2: 1st Principle of Momentum: Agility Through Analytics—Far from the static marketing campaigns of the past, the new ecosystem demands agile marketing based on analytics. This chapter will show you how to lay the groundwork for agility, introduce the most helpful analytics tools, and demonstrate exactly how to tweak your marketing strategy to drive results.

Chapter 3: 2nd Principle of Momentum: Customer Focus—The new marketing ecosystem is completely customer-driven, from its reliance on customer engagement and feedback to its focus on customization. But perhaps most importantly, the most successful digital marketing today enables consumer self-expression. This chapter will show you how to craft your marketing strategy to attract your ideal customers and make them into fans for life.

Chapter 4: 3rd Principle of Momentum: Integration—Marketing today no longer occurs via individual, siloed media. Rather, customers interact with you simultaneously via multiple channels, both physical and digital. This chapter will discuss ways to merge your strategies for individual channels into one cohesive whole.

Chapter 5: 4th Principle of Momentum: Content Curation—The old model of marketing demanded content in high quantities. The new model focuses on quality and smart content curation—filtering the content you share through your unique brand. This chapter will show you how to become a pro at attracting visitors—and ultimately, customers—with your approach to content.

Chapter 6: 5th Principle of Momentum: Cross-Pollination—Every resource you have can be harnessed to give your marketing more momentum, and this chapter will show you how. From leveraging relationships with employees, vendors, and partners, to integrating every aspect of your business under the marketing umbrella, you'll learn how to move from scattered to strategic in your use of the assets available to you.

The final chapter, **Chapter 7: Measuring Marketing ROI in the Digital Age**, will focus on how to measure marketing ROI in this new ecosystem. In today's multi-touch marketing world, are you mistaking the final touch point as the only point of conversion? You have to make sure that you are considering the multi-faceted nature of today's marketing as you measure ROI.

Making the change from the old model of marketing to the new ecosystem of momentum doesn't have to be difficult. In fact, as you make the transition, you'll see right away how much easier it is to handle than the old model, with its constant push for more content and more posts on more social media platforms. So take a deep breath, let go of your current notions of marketing, and let's dive into the new reality of digital marketing together.

chapter **2**

1st Principle of Momentum:
Agility Through Analytics

Agility means the ability to pivot and change direction quickly, based on data gained from in-depth analytics, in order to take advantage of opportunities to grow your business. Your business' marketing momentum depends heavily on its ability to embrace agility and continuously revamp its strategies based on analytics.

HOW MANY TIMES have you heard the business mantra "Adapt or die"? It's a common enough saying that you'd think this first principle of momentum, agility, was nothing new. The imperative to change according to market conditions has always been a major part of business.

But what hasn't always been a part of business is the incredible amount of data now available, from supply-chain tracking information to e-commerce website analytics.

Due to this constant influx of data, adapting is no longer something that can take place only every once in a while—every few years, say, or even every quarter. Today agile businesses can, and should, adapt to changing conditions and new information almost instantly.

The sheer volume of data available in real time about every aspect of consumers' interactions with your emails, social media posts, blog posts, website, and paid ads means that shaping and refining strategies and campaigns based on that information is a never-ending process.

And that process is the single most essential element in capitalizing on and building momentum from your marketing successes.

In the world of digital marketing, things happen at the speed of light. A well-timed tweet can go viral in seconds, spreading brand awareness in no time flat—think Oreo's famous tweet when the lights went out at the Super Bowl in 2013: "Power out? No problem. You can still dunk in the dark." It's that kind of swift move to take advantage of a trending topic or a new insight into audience behavior that creates the momentum you need to be successful in today's marketing ecosystem—and it's the constant tweaks and course adjustments, based on data about your audience's responses to your marketing, that continue to build that momentum.

Agility in marketing leads directly to marketing momentum. So how can your company go about becoming more agile?

» Agility in Action

Let's take another look at that sports drink company we mentioned in chapter 1—we'll call them Marketade. How did Marketade come up with the idea to promote its drinks through mobile and Facebook offers? Did Stan in Marketing just come up with the brilliant idea during a meeting one day, all fleshed out and ready to implement?

Yeah, probably not.

The idea probably began as a much simpler version of the promotion, maybe just an offer for a free drink popping up once a jogger reached the end of their route.

Now, Marketade is an agile company, so it tracks its analytics carefully, and then puts its insights to good use.

In looking at the data here, Stan probably noticed that their initial offer was successful, and that customers weren't waiting to redeem it, but instead were going to the nearest store to immediately get their free drink. But even more exciting than that, *they were then sharing the fact that they had gotten a free drink with friends on social media!*

Had anyone asked them to share this information? Nope. Did they get any benefit from telling friends? No. And yet there they were, letting their friends know about the promotion. What gives?

People love to spread the word about deals among friends—especially when associating themselves with a certain product or service makes them look good. And what could possibly make you look better than sharing a deal on a healthy drink, thus subtly letting friends know how fit and health-conscious you are?

Stan realized that Marketade was really on to something here. How could they tweak the campaign to capitalize on the momentum that was already building through these voluntary shares?

First, Stan decided to make immediate offer redemption part of the deal. So many people were already doing it on their own that making it mandatory might just inspire the rest to do so, too. The offer was then linked to stores near the ends of the joggers' routes to make it an easy yes. This first tweak strengthened the momentum already building.

Next, Stan added a step that customers were already taking on their own—but made it even more attractive, so that more of them would participate by offering another discount for friends when a jogger posted a selfie on Facebook with their free drink. In the process, Marketade capitalized on our love affair with selfies as well as our desire to associate ourselves with products that make us look good and our excitement about sharing great deals with friends.

The result? Marketing gold. Stan's tweaks to the campaign really only took what customers were already doing and made it a standard part of the deal, but by tapping into what people were willing to do anyway and attaching a reward to it, he increased the momentum of the campaign dramatically.

If Stan hadn't been checking his analytics religiously, he wouldn't have known about the customer response until it was too late to take advantage of it. But by listening and observing and tracking, he was able to make his campaign into something much more effective than it ever could have been in its original form.

That is agility.

That is marketing momentum.

» Growth Hacking: Agility on Steroids

You may have heard the term *growth hacking* being thrown around the internet in recent years. What is it, exactly?

Growth hacking is an extreme version of agility tactics. It is a method used by many tech startups that burst onto the scene with a vengeance, disrupting their industry by growing from literally nothing to a thriving business in as little time as possible.

Unlike established companies, these growth hackers don't feel bound by conventional marketing methods, and they don't try to meet a long list of marketing goals—instead, they look for uniquely creative ways to get as much as possible out of their marketing efforts, and obsess over one thing and one thing only: growth. They scrutinize analytics constantly, and make major changes instantly based on trends and insights gleaned from those analytics, to amp up results. Focus is key in growth hacking—every single move is based on data and aimed at growth. It's the perfect marriage of left-brain and right-brain, creativity and science. And this uber-emphasis on agility means that growth-hacking companies can sometimes go from 0 to 60 in just a few weeks—the momentum produced can be almost unbelievable.

New businesses in other industries can use these tactics, too, as can established companies, with just a little tweaking to accommodate needs other than growth alone.

Here's a real-world example:

A Fortune 500 client of ours was launching a new educational app for kids. It enabled kids to practice math and English skills they needed more help on, as well as work ahead of their grade level for enrichment. It displayed results to parents, so they could keep track of their children's progress, and could even be synced up with input from teachers and used by school systems. All in all, it was a really exciting new tool for kids, parents, and educators alike.

The client wanted to make a big splash, so the Marketing Zen team decided to use growth-hacking techniques to reach the client's ambitious goals for explosive growth.

First, we set up a killer landing page, designed with one simple conversion in mind—capturing people's email addresses. We kept it focused, with minimal text, a strong call to action, a design centered around the sign-up field, and a short demo video. This landing page was our cornerstone, our growth-hacking focus. We wanted email addresses so that we would have a huge audience of excited potential users to contact as soon as the app launched.

Next, we set up social media accounts for the brand, and started an intensive campaign to spread brand awareness among our target audiences. We ran paid ads on Facebook targeting moms, in order to gain fans for the Facebook page, get our name in front of them, and drive them to the landing page. We researched influential mommy bloggers and educational gurus, and followed them on Twitter, in order to encourage them to follow us in return, to make them aware of our existence, and to drive them to the landing page.

Then, we started an influencer outreach campaign, building strategic relationships with some of those mommy bloggers and influencers in the field of education, and offering to write guest blogs on their sites. Posts we wrote for them reached their audiences and others, as we also shared them on Stumbleupon via paid ads. In fact, one post went viral on Stumbleupon, getting reblogged over and over again. In every guest post was a link to the landing page.

But that's only where the campaign *started*. Every step of the way, we kept one eye glued to the analytics. When we saw that traffic was hitting the landing page, but not converting at the rates we wanted, we tweaked the text and design and even added special offers in return for signing up, until we had created a veritable conversion machine. When we realized how effective our outreach strategy was in generating new traffic to the landing page, we sweetened the deal for influencers in order to get more of them on board, offering them exclusive deals and early access.

Nothing was sacred. Everything was susceptible to change if the analytics so dictated. And thanks to our growth-hacking tactics, our pre-launch campaign built up a sizeable email subscriber list and kept them excited through regular email updates, continued activity on social media, and outreach, so that even before the app launched, its momentum was already substantial—and it's still growing.

The radical agility practiced by growth hackers clearly demonstrates the link between analytics, agility, and marketing momentum.

» Your Turn

So how can your company make the switch to an agile marketing mindset?

As we saw above, it's all about the analytics.

But before you can start using analytics to inform your marketing strategies, you first need to assess your current situation, define targets and goals, and create an overall plan. Otherwise, you won't know what you're aiming for or whether your efforts are having the effect you want them to.

With that in mind, here is how to lay the necessary groundwork for agility in your business:

1. Start with a clean slate, assessing absolutely everything in your current marketing strategy with a critical eye.

If you truly want to embrace agility, you'll need to let go of some things you've grown used to—or even attached to—in your current marketing strategy. Assume the mindset of a complete stranger, a consultant coming in and seeing your marketing strategy for the very first time. What does your overall strategy look like currently? What are all the moving parts? What have your results been like, both for individual campaigns and channels, and overall? Why do you do the things you currently do?

» Business X (let's say they're an IT solutions provider) has used the same basic strategy for years. They put their website in place, optimized it for search, and have pretty much left it alone since they built it. They do have a blog, updated regularly and enthusiastically by an employee who treats it a lot more like a personal blog than a company blog, rambling about his views on various topics rather than creating actual marketing content. They send out email newsletters to their customers and prospects every so often—not really on a regular basis, but as often as they can get to it. And they have a presence on Facebook, Twitter, and LinkedIn, since they heard that every business worth its salt these days had to have social media accounts—but rarely have the time to post.

The results of their digital marketing efforts have been lackluster. Their site gets some traffic, but most deals are still made via the same old outbound techniques their salespeople have been using for years, cold calling chief among them. Their newsletters don't seem to have much of an effect, unless they announce a sale or deal, and their social media accounts sit mostly idle. Their blog is popular with its writer's friends and family, but doesn't seem to attract many other visitors—or more importantly, any leads.

Basically, they are online because you have to be in order to be taken seriously. And with a pretty much nonexistent ROI from their inbound marketing, they felt they couldn't really justify the amount of resources it would take to keep up with everything on a regular basis.

When Business X took a good look at their current strategy, they realized that they didn't really have a solid "why" behind most of the things they did. They also admitted to themselves that they had been checking analytics only sporadically, and certainly not taking any action based on the data, other than growing frustrated with the few resources they were putting towards marketing.

> ## A COMPANY GETTING IT RIGHT
>
> Business operations and customer relations software company SAP is a multinational behemoth that's been known and respected the world over for more than forty years—and is a great example of a large enterprise fully embracing the concept of agility and establishing a robust testing and optimization program.
>
> In 2009 SAP VP Shawn Burns set about creating enterprise web analytics at the company to replace a disparate set of analytics tools then in use in various divisions of the very large organization. Six months into the process of getting all of SAP's business data and analytics "under one roof," so to speak, Burns had a realization—he understood that just having all that data in one place wasn't maximizing its value. What SAP needed was to, as Burns put it, get "a process and dedicated team" that would focus on the data "to squeeze the value out of it."
>
> The result of Burns's epiphany was the creation of SAP's Test Lab, a dedicated testing and optimization team that, since its creation, has run tests and optimized elements across SAP's marketing efforts in different channels and even different global marketplaces.
>
> SAP's Test Lab keeps an organized queue of tests to be performed that are ranked by value to the company, knowing that the Test Lab is a finite corporate resource. The team also keeps documentation to preserve institutional knowledge

gained from every test. Now the team runs around twenty-five tests each quarter.

Why such a limited number of tests? The Test Lab's goal is continual improvement and optimization, and their team is willing to run multiple iterations on specific testing areas, such as visual imagery in marketing material, to fully optimize results for each element in a given test.

2. Identify your business goals.

Of course you're already aware of your company's overall goals. But listing them out on paper puts them in the forefront of your mind, and will allow you to refer back to them easily while working on your marketing plan. Every aspect of your marketing strategy should be directly traceable back to your overall goals as a business—otherwise, you're wasting resources.

» Business X's list of overall goals: To increase sales by a specific percentage each year. To reach more prospects, create brand awareness, and establish themselves as industry leaders. To boost the number of clients who enter into long-term consultative contracts, rather just buying a solution in a one-time transaction.

3. Identify your conversion goals.

What exactly does "conversion" mean to you—in the context of your overall marketing strategy, as well as in the context of each channel and campaign you plan to use? Maybe you want sales—okay, good. But maybe you're after email addresses instead (or also!), or likes on Facebook, or something entirely different. That's fine, too—the important thing is that you define what you want up front and make sure these goals are measurable and trackable. Email addresses and Facebook likes can be counted; "brand awareness" is a more nebulous goal.

» Business X's old marketing strategy had a vague focus on brand awareness and attracting leads, but nothing really quantifiable. Instead of actively targeting specific conversions, they had simply been going through the motions—doing the blog, doing social media—without any concrete purpose in mind.

They set a new conversion goal: gathering email addresses to market to. Now, all digital marketing efforts would be aimed at reaching a wider audience through thought leadership, and then gathering as many email addresses from that new audience as possible, in order to add prospects to their email subscriber list. That way, they could begin moving them through the sales funnel, directing them towards the specific relationship Business X wanted to have with them.

4. Quick Check: Do your conversion goals correspond with the stated goals of your business?

Take a look at what you're striving for online and whether it matches up with your real-world goals for your company. Getting Facebook likes is all well and good, but if it's not leading to more sales of your gadgets, and that's your goal, then you need to rethink what you consider a conversion online. If your real-world goal is building a larger audience of warm leads to market to, then collecting email addresses should be first and foremost.

» For Business X, email marketing was the digital marketing channel that they felt would be most effective at helping them reach their overall business goal of lead nurturing. Therefore, all other efforts would now ultimately be geared towards persuading people to share their email addresses.

5. Define your target profiles.

Next, you want to figure out who it is you're targeting with your online marketing efforts. Get specific—not just "women," but "married women with kids, between the ages of thirty and forty-five, who make more than $50,000 a year and like animals." Come up with at least three different customer personas for your ideal customers, focusing on demographics, interests, and pain points, then research where those people hang out online and what speaks to them there.

» Business X already had a very in-depth understanding of the kinds of business customers it wanted to target. What it didn't know, however, was how to reach those people online. So the marketing department did some research into which social media platforms their customers used most heavily—Facebook? Twitter? LinkedIn? Instagram? Pinterest?—and what sort of content they engaged with while there. They looked at what sorts of blog posts and email newsletters truly interested their target audience, and what kind of resources they wanted to see on an IT solutions provider's website. They polled their current customers, asked prospects, searched for industry conversations happening on social media, and drew up complete profiles that detailed where and how to reach the exact people they wanted to reach online.

They found that their target audience mostly hung out on LinkedIn and Twitter, and appreciated industry-related information—tips for choosing an IT solution, for example, or explanations of how various solutions could help with different issues.

6. Create an overall digital marketing strategy.

Based on the above goals and information, develop your new strategy. It may be similar to your existing one, or it may be completely different. The key is that you now have specific goals to work toward, the results of which are measurable and based on concrete data. You'll determine which channels you'll use and what type of content you'll create based on your target audience's preferences. You'll decide which conversion goals to pursue, based on your overall business goals.

» Since Business X's overarching marketing goal was to gain email addresses for email marketing, all other marketing activities had to be geared towards that end. So social media campaigns needed to entice people to click through to a landing page that collected their email address. The website needed to give visitors the chance to share their email on every page. And even the email newsletter going out to current subscribers needed to ask them to forward it to a friend who might find it useful, in the hopes that they might subscribe, too.

7. Develop individual marketing campaigns and initiatives.

Within your new strategy, you can now finally begin to create individual campaigns. Again, these should all be geared towards driving the specific, quantifiable conversions you've decided on, which should all contribute clearly to your larger business goals.

» Business X decided they would post educational blog posts filled with useful industry information on LinkedIn on a regular basis, as well as taking an active part in the conversations in relevant LinkedIn Groups. They also planned to create a free e-book containing valuable information for their target audience, promote it on Twitter, and give it away to anyone who subscribed to their emails. And they decided to start updating their website with new, search-friendly content, in order to attract more prospects via Google.

8. Realize that the marketing strategy and campaigns you just spent so much time on will need to change—many times.

You already know this, but knowing something and really being ready and willing to do it are two different things. In order to become an agile marketer, you've got to be truly willing to make changes—sometimes tiny, sometimes drastic—based on what you see in your analytics. And not just once, but over and over again—every single time you see something that needs to be acted on. Creating a strategy is not a one-and-done–type thing. Your strategy and campaigns will need constant tweaking.

» Business X committed to thinking of each change they would make as the next step in an ongoing process, not as revisiting something that had been finished.

9. Don't expect instant results.

Unless you're a growth hacker looking for instant results from an intensive marketing push, it's not just okay but *necessary* to give your strategy some time to work. Don't get worried if orders don't start pouring in immediately once you publish that blog post, or if no one has signed up for your webinar yet, even though you sent the email yesterday. Look at what's happening week by week, and often even month by month, to see where trends are emerging and where changes need to be made. As a general rule of thumb, the newer your online marketing strategy is, the more time it will need to work. A company that's brand new to blogging or to social media might not see results for ninety days or even longer, while a company simply making tweaks to an existing strategy might start seeing results within a week.

» Business X decided to look at their analytics on a daily basis in order to see what was taking off and what was not so successful, but determined that they would hold back for at least ninety days and give their campaigns a chance to work rather than get frustrated and change things too soon.

10. Put things in motion, and then fan the flames.

Take action on your campaigns, and start watching your analytics. Now that the groundwork has been laid for agile, analytics-driven marketing, the real work begins. This is where you monitor, analyze, and then tweak, over and over again, until you have optimized and fine-tuned your campaigns and your strategy to achieve their highest possible levels of success. This is where you find out where the momentum is slowly beginning to build in your marketing efforts, and then fan the flames by adding more and more fuel to those successful areas.

» Business X launched its campaigns, and then saw that their conversations in LinkedIn Groups were having a real effect on quality traffic coming to their site, so they decided to ramp up their efforts in that area. They also noticed that traffic from search was still not as high as they wanted it to be, so they decided to try paid ads on Google as well. They discovered that Twitter posts that included an image were significantly more effective at driving traffic to the site to subscribe than those without, so they created images to attract more attention. The constant tweaks paid off in more conversions—more email addresses—which in turn meant that overall business goals were being reached.

» Analytics Tools

Tracking all this data sounds complicated, but there are plenty of tools you can use to keep tabs on it all. When it comes to analytics, however, there's no one-size-fits-all tool that tracks every piece of data on every platform. So it's important to understand what types of tools are available, and how to combine them to get the best insight into your audience's behavior.

The analytics tool that should have the most direct and noticeable impact on your day-to-day marketing activities and campaigns is *marketing automation software*. This branch of business software covers a very wide range of capabilities, although the term typically is used to define software that helps marketers to:

- collect and track data, often across multiple channels
- organize and sort that data to make database segmentation much easier when creating targeted campaigns
- actually help execute marketing campaigns, while tracking the progress and results of those efforts

Here's a (very) limited list of marketing automation technology vendors, ranging from email-specific tools to full marketing automation suites that cover everything from email statistics to social media analytics to lead-generation tools. Some are better suited for smaller businesses, some are highly scalable and appeal to both SMB (small- and medium-size businesses) and enterprise companies, and others probably are best described as enterprise-class. But all are established in the marketing industry.

- **AWeber:** Affordable and easy-to-use email marketing and analytics, perfect for smaller businesses.
- **MailChimp:** Intuitive email marketing and data tracking, great for beginners.
- **Constant Contact:** Designed to help small businesses and nonprofits grow through analytics and automation of marketing tasks such as email.

- **Infusionsoft:** Exclusively for small businesses; offers lead generation tools and marketing automation, as well as email and social media tools.
- **Silverpop:** Offers simple marketing automation and email marketing solutions for mid-size to large enterprises.
- **Return Path:** Sees data as the key to building relationships and helps marketers build those relationships effortlessly through marketing automation.
- **Oracle:** A pioneer in the industry: optimizes the entire marketing process, from lead capture to completed deal; ideal for large businesses.
- **Aprimo:** Focuses on integration of all aspects of marketing automation software; perfect for enterprises looking to integrate their efforts.
- **HubSpot:** All-in-one marketing platform to track analytics and optimize marketing efforts, making complex marketing easy for large businesses.
- **Pardot:** Automated support for the longer timespan and multi-step decisions involved in B2B (business-to-business) sales.
- **Marketo:** Includes marketing automation, social marketing, lead nurturing, budget management, analytics, sales insight, and website personalization—just right for large businesses needing all the bells and whistles.

The next piece in the analytics pie is *website statistics tools.* Any discussion of analytics tools, website statistics tools in particular, has to mention Google Analytics. It is free to use and provides a wealth of information on website traffic and visitor behavior.

Here, for example, are four categories Google Analytics uses to calculate results metrics:

- **Content:** How many times was a particular page viewed?
- **Goals:** Which pages' URLs contributed to the highest goal conversion rate?
- **E-commerce:** How much value did a given page contribute to a transaction?
- **Internal search:** Which internal search terms contributed to a transaction?

On top of the free analytical tool itself, Google also provides free educational courses and free online help forums, so users can learn how to make the most out of the tool's features.

For marketers looking for even more in-depth analysis than Google Analytics can provide, there are also enterprise-class analytics tools available that collect more data and allow for more customized metrics reporting. In addition, there are data collection and analysis tools that specifically drill into social media platforms and metrics. (See the list of integration tools in chapter 4.)

Combining a website analytics tool with a social media tool and metrics from marketing automation technology provides a complete overview of your digital marketing data, and allows you to track and measure your campaigns and marketing strategy.

Testing is also a vital part of tweaking your campaigns to make them more effective. Why put just one web page or email out there to collect data on, when you can get twice as much data from two? Creating two versions—called split testing or A/B testing—gives you the ability to more easily and quickly compare what's working and what's not, and then make changes to your campaign as necessary. Some marketing automation software suites have *testing tools* built into their feature set, and there are also software packages that handle A/B tests, from the technical elements of executing the tests to keeping track of statistical significance to ensure you are making informed decisions in your ongoing testing and optimization program that is based on meaningful data.

Google Analytics offers some testing tools for landing pages, and Google AdWords has testing tools for paid search ads. Here is a short list of some enterprise-class testing technology available:

- **Optimizely:** Allows you to run A/B and multivariate tests on web and mobile content in order to help you determine which version delivers the best possible customer experience, and thus more conversions.
- **Maxymiser:** Affiliated with Oracle, the only tool that enables A/B and multivariate testing on the entire multi-channel customer sales funnel.
- **Adobe Test&Target:** Focuses on customizing experiences for your customers through testing that determines how best to personalize content for each one.

- **Kissmetrics:** Provides testing tools that supply customer intelligence to help you understand your users, so that you can better cater to their preferences and behavior online.
- **Unbounce:** Focuses on helping you create high-converting landing pages through testing.
- **Visual Website Optimizer:** Bills itself as the world's easiest split testing tool for websites.

» Agile Analytics Tips

Every business is unique, and so every strategy and every campaign will be unique. But you should be looking at many of the same types of analytics no matter what—and you'll want to respond to what those analytics tell you in broadly similar ways. Here's a game plan for some of the most common analytics findings:

1. Balance your traffic sources.

When you look at a pie chart showing which percentage of your website traffic came from where, take note of those traffic sources and their different percentages. The prevailing wisdom in the online marketing industry is that, as a general rule of thumb, you want to balance out your traffic sources so that about 40 percent come from organic search, 20 percent from direct traffic, 20 percent from referring sites, and 10 percent from campaigns. If a higher percentage is finding you through searches, you're a little too exposed to Google's algorithm changes—if the next Google update ends up penalizing sites for something you happen to be doing, you stand to lose a dangerous amount of your traffic. If you're getting fewer than 20 percent of your visitors from direct traffic, you may need to do more offline advertising. If fewer than 20 percent of your visitors come from referring sites, you may need to up your blogging outreach and social media sharing. And if fewer than 10 percent come from your campaigns, you need to rethink how those campaigns are structured, since the ultimate goal of every campaign should be to drive traffic to your site.

2. Look at repeat visits to understand customer behavior.

Repeat visitors are the ones you've hooked, and you want to know what you did right to get them to come back so that you can be sure to do more of it! Look at the length and depth of their visits, as well as how far apart those visits were spaced, to see what they're doing on your site and when. Which pages are they visiting? That will show you what they like—and what they probably want to see more of.

3. Look for your most frequently visited pages and make more like them.

It only makes sense that if customers keep coming back for certain types of pages, you should keep them happy by creating more of the same. Those pages are the ones that have proven to be most effective for you—why wouldn't you make more just like them? If recipes featuring your products bring people back, keep posting new ones. If your customers like to read educational content about your industry, keep it coming.

4. Look for landing pages that are not working.

If landing pages for campaigns aren't producing results, you've got to figure out why, and fix it. Maybe the wrong people are being targeted by your campaign—in which case you need to rethink that campaign. Or maybe something about the page itself is poor—the content is lacking, or the design is confusing. Whatever the reason, you need to find it—and change it.

5. Pay attention to which traffic source provides you with visitors who stay the longest and who do what you want them to do.

Balancing your traffic sources is important, but so is capitalizing on your successes. Maybe you have a ton of traffic coming from search—but they hardly ever buy. On the other hand, you have only a few visitors coming in from your campaigns—but they always end up staying a long time and usually buy something! Accordingly, you should focus on ramping up your campaigns to bring in more of those buyers and on tweaking your search engine optimization (SEO) strategy to draw in higher quality traffic.

6. Check data about abandoned carts and forms.

Many marketers forget to check and see at which point people abandon their carts or stop filling out a form. Maybe once they see how much shipping is, they balk. Or maybe it's because you don't accept PayPal—or because PayPal is your only method of payment. Maybe the form just gets annoying after the third or fourth unnecessary question. Check to see where you're losing people, and fix it.

7. Check heat map reporting and analytics.

Where do people click on your pages? If your site is well designed, the organization of your pages will guide readers' eyes to the places you want them to go. Visitors will find it easy to follow the path they need, and click where you'd like them to click. But if things are too confusing, they might click around randomly for a bit and then leave, frustrated.

8. Confirm that your calls to action are working.

If you're asking a customer to do something, you want them to do it. If they are, you've got it right—but if they're not clicking or downloading or buying, your call to action needs to be tweaked.

9. Look for the most effective content on your website, and make more content like it.

These aren't necessarily the pages that are visited most often (item #3 above)—they're the ones that lead visitors to buy, or whatever else it is you want your visitors to do, whether that's downloading something or signing up for something. Once you identify content that's converting, have your other content imitate it.

10. Make tag clouds out of the search keywords driving traffic to your site to see if the keywords that bring people there are appropriate to your content and marketing goals.

This one is fun *and* useful! Take the keywords people used to find your site, go to www.wordle.net, and create a tag cloud with them. This will give you an instant visual of which words dominate searches that lead to your website, and which don't. Adjust your keyword strategy accordingly, by creating more site content focused around the keywords you actually want to be found for.

11. Make tag clouds out of your internal search keywords, too.

You can do the same thing with searches on your site to see what visitors have been looking for, and then use that info to spark blog content ideas or create new products.

12. Look at your conversions campaign by campaign to save money.

Don't lump all your campaigns together when looking at your results. Instead, review each one individually. Maybe a hashtag you've created on Twitter is going gangbusters, but a product giveaway campaign on Facebook is just meh. Save resources by cutting the campaigns that aren't working, and focusing your efforts on the ones that are.

13. Find your site's exit points.

Maybe visitors come to your site, read a blog post or two, and then leave. Or maybe they read a blog post, read your

"About Me" page, look at your products for a few seconds, and then leave. If they're leaving without buying, you want to know why. Which page lost their interest? Find it and fix it.

14. Use bounce rate information to optimize pages.

If visitors are bouncing from certain pages—leaving your site almost as soon as they arrive, without visiting any other pages—you need to fix those landing pages. Which ones make them leave? Which ones don't? Experiment with changes in content and appearance until bounce rates are reduced.

15. Be alert for unknowns in your data.

Check for alerts in your analytics. If there was an unexplained spike or dip in your activity, try to figure out why. What was happening during that time period? And how can you re-create or avoid that later?

16. Scale up your efforts on traffic sources that are doing well.

If you're getting a lot of people from your social media campaigns, start working those campaigns even harder. Same goes for if you're getting quality traffic from referral sites, or even searches, if you're building that up as a source—do more of what's working.

17. Test different versions of web pages and emails—even blog titles and email subject lines.

If you're not sure what approach to take on a certain page or in a certain email, but have a few options, try split-testing them with a small portion of your audience, and then use the resulting data to decide what to use for the rest of your audience.

One final thing to remember: No individual tip is as important as looking at how everything you do online interacts with everything else. All of your company's online activities should be integrated. Your website, your social media, your blog, your paid ads—it's all interconnected. What you do in one place will affect what happens in the others, and vice versa. Look at your online marketing strategy as a whole, rather than as a bunch of segmented pieces, and you'll be ahead of the game.

The only path to agility is through analytics. By focusing on your goals, continuously tracking your results, and then tweaking your campaigns to take advantage of trends, you can fan the flames of momentum building around your marketing efforts and maximize their effects. It's not about sticking to a plan anymore—it's about pivoting instantly as need dictates.

Chapter 2 Takeaways

» Agility is the first principle of momentum.
» Agility means making frequent adjustments to your marketing strategy and campaigns based on data gleaned from analytics.
» Growth hacking takes agility to the extreme, in order to produce incredible marketing momentum.
» In order to become agile, you must first lay the groundwork by assessing your current marketing situation, defining goals and targets, and developing a new strategy.

» Analytics tools like marketing automation software, website analytics, social media analytics, and testing software are vital in your pursuit of agility.

» Certain trends in the data of your analytics call for certain specific changes to be made to your strategy—putting the right tweak in place at the right time is crucial to building momentum.

chapter **3**

2nd Principle of Momentum:
Customer Focus

Customer focus means identifying who your customers are, listening to (and acting on) their input and feedback, and personalizing their experience with your company. Being customer focused
means being a brand whose values your customer wants to be
associated with. Building marketing momentum through customer
focus is just a matter of putting the customer in charge.

L IKE AGILITY, a focus on the customer isn't exactly a revo-
lutionary idea, on the face of it. Of course businesses focus
on their customers—how else would they make any money?
Why else would businesses spend millions on focus groups
and incentivize customer surveys? The customer is king, and
always has been! An obsession with customers is the heart of
a business' success.

But in the old model, no matter how much customer input
was sought, and no matter how much a specific demographic
was catered to, all marketing was, in the end, company-led,
not customer-led.

Companies decided how they would market to their customers. Companies determined the brand experience that each customer would have. Companies developed the messaging they wanted customers to receive. Every aspect of companies' marketing was tightly controlled.

Through the power of the internet, however, all of that changed. With the advent of Facebook and Twitter, review sites, and influencer blogging, customers suddenly had a public forum to speak their minds about products and services, and broadcast their opinions and experiences to huge audiences. Word of mouth was a powerful marketing force before the internet—now, magnified exponentially because of the sheer numbers that online content could reach, it had an even more dramatic effect. The balance of power shifted; an individual's online comments about a brand could have more of an effect on the way that company was perceived than even the most carefully crafted marketing campaign. This loss of control over their brands' images meant that companies had to rethink their entire approach to marketing.

As a graduate student at the University of Texas at Austin, I did my thesis on Twitter (. . . no, it wasn't in 140 characters). I was enthralled with understanding social media. One of the pivotal questions of my thesis was this: Why do people use social networking sites? My (incorrect) hypothesis was that people wanted to connect to each other. But my research revealed that this was only the secondary reason. The primary reason was to showcase their own identity.

I'll pause while you reflect for a moment on the narcissism of society. Then, I'll urge you to think deeper. We, as humans, have always had an innate need to express ourselves. By that very expression, we craft our identity.

Smart companies, such as Facebook (with their timeline feature) and Amazon (with their personalized recommendations), are already taking advantage of what I refer to as an Identity-Based Ecosystem. The digital world of tomorrow, be it consumer or business, will revolve around the identity of the individual. To succeed, companies will have to be proactive about harnessing the idea that showcasing our identity is the most human and primary of desires.

The question companies asked used to be: What does our brand say about us? Today the question needs to be: What does doing business with us allow our customers to say about themselves?

Today, every single marketing move a customer-focused company makes is dictated by the customer. The starting point of every strategy must be the customer's perspective, not the company's. Through the analytics and testing we discussed in the last chapter, businesses work to discover who their customers are, what kinds of content they actively seek out and want to engage with and share, how and where and when they want to be marketed to, which values they want to be seen to espouse, and what types of brand experiences they get excited about. This laser-like focus on the customer produces uniquely strong marketing momentum—because who doesn't love a deal tailored to their exact preferences?

So how does this change in focus play out in an actual marketing campaign? Let's peek into the inner workings of Marketade again to find out.

» Customer Focus in Action

We've already heard all about how Stan from Marketing tweaked Marketade's free drink campaign based on analytics, finding the areas where momentum was building naturally and making changes in those areas in order to fan the flames. But we never did find out where the original idea for a free drink at the end of a jogger's route came from.

For this brilliant idea, Marketade had Savanna (also from Marketing) to thank. Savanna was the force behind the company's intensive push to become customer-focused. She spent not just days, not just weeks, but months online, listening to customers' social media conversations, reading relevant blogs, and delving into the data about Marketade's online audience.

Once she had put together a pretty solid picture of the demographics of Marketade's customers, their interests, values, and habits, whose blogs they read, where they liked to hang out online, and what they liked to do there, Savanna created a few different customer personas to embody what she had learned.

For example, there was "Annie," a thirty-something mom who spent most of her time online connecting with other moms on Facebook, was into fitness- and health-related blogs, often shared posts with friends on social media, and was in a moms' jogging club that kept in touch via Facebook, sharing their jogging routes and successes using their Fitbits.

Then there was "Bryan," a single guy in his late twenties, who was into business leadership and fitness in equal measures. His social media posts consisted mainly of links to business-related or fitness-related content, with occasional selfies taken on various fitness adventures—rock-climbing, kayaking—thrown in, as well. Bryan was no fitness novice: He was into the nitty-gritty details of dietary supplements and the latest workout trends.

Using these two customer personas, Savanna was then able to imagine what types of marketing campaigns would be most appealing to Marketade's customer base. Putting herself in Annie's shoes, she realized that Annie wanted to be seen as a health- and fitness-conscious mom by her circle of friends—and not only that, but one who helped those friends on their own journeys to healthier living. This was the image of herself she projected through Facebook posts and the values that were important to her. In order to market to Annie effectively, Marketade needed to provide Annie with the opportunity to make that statement about herself to her friends, and give her a way to help them, as well.

Putting herself in Bryan's shoes, Savanna saw that Bryan understood the importance of refueling with the right dietary supplement at the right time—and would also value convenience in his nonstop businessman's day.

With these two goals in mind, Savanna created the offer: At the end of a jogging route, a free sports drink. Annie, with her group of jogging moms, would probably delight in telling her friends about her connection with Marketade, bring the entire group to the store with her—where they might all buy drinks—and then share the story with other friends online, as well. For Bryan, the convenience and timing of the offer would make rehydrating irresistible.

What's more, both Annie and Bryan would experience the offer as a personalized deal just for them, since it would be presented to them at the end of their unique jogging route. That personal touch would make it more likely that they would feel that the company was reaching out to them on an individual level—an approach that would make anyone feel special.

Once Savanna launched the campaign, Stan, as you'll recall, took over, adding his own analytics-based tweaks—which continued to speak to these customer personas. Sharing selfies with the drink in order to spread the deal to her friends was a no-brainer for Annie, who loved to be seen as associated with such a healthy brand, and loved to help her friends just as much. For Bryan, the selfie appealed to his sense of leadership—it allowed him to share insider fitness deals with his followers—as well as his desire to be viewed as serious about fitness.

Everything about this campaign was customer-focused, from its inception to its various iterations. Where before, marketers would have decided what message to broadcast to customers, now, brands listen to customers to determine what message customers want to broadcast about themselves, and craft marketing strategy around that desire. Old-school marketers would use the same campaign—and even overall strategy—for every customer, while successful marketers in the digital age segment their campaigns, sometimes even to the point of individualizing them for each customer.

The customer is not just king—the customer is the foundation for a whole new marketing approach, and the impetus that gets—and keeps—the marketing momentum going.

» **Going Viral: Customer Focus at Its Best**

When a video or other piece of content begins to spread well beyond expectations, you know you've got marketing gold. But what is it that makes a campaign go viral? Sure, sometimes it's just the luck of the draw, a funny video that happens to get shared by the right people at the right times. But a more dependable way to cause a campaign to go viral is to make it personal. Tap into the emotions of the customer, make them feel that you understand them and that they are important to you, and your campaign will spread itself.

One example? The ALS Ice Bucket Challenge. By focusing on their audience as opposed to themselves, the association managed to raise hundreds of millions of dollars for ALS research. Since individuals were challenged to create their own videos, the campaign became personal, and tapped into everyone's innate desire to do good—and the desire to be *seen* doing good.

Another example of a marketing campaign going viral is one the Marketing Zen team put together for a client of ours. This client sells call-center software for 911 dispatch centers— programs that help train dispatchers, record calls, and make response times more efficient. Its customers are the managers of those dispatch centers: the people who work with their team of dispatchers every day, spend their time training and supporting them, are good friends with them, and who probably were once dispatchers themselves.

So when we started brainstorming ideas for a campaign that could go viral for our client, we made it personal. What would grip the hearts of dispatchers and their supervisors alike? How could our client show its customers that they understood them and were on their side?

We decided to write a tribute to 911 dispatchers, from the first-person perspective. Here's just a part of what we came up with:

I am a 911 dispatcher.

I am the one who responds when you call out for help.

I am the one who walks with you, hand-in-hand and step-by-step, during the most frightening events in your life.

But you'll probably never meet me.

I deliver babies. I administer CPR. I shield people from violence. I put out fires. I catch criminals.

I save lives.

I care so much that I have nightmares about the screams. I care so much that I will never forget the fear, the panic, the pain in people's voices. I care so much that when I get home, I can't help but cry over the suffering in the world, and my helplessness to stop it.

Except that I'm not helpless.

I am a 911 dispatcher.

I am strong.

I am the refuge people fly to when they are in danger. I am the fortress holding back the darkness. I am the guardian angel who guides people through catastrophe unseen.

I am a 911 dispatcher.

And I am proud.

I also know what it is to be ignored by the public, and even to be shouted at, cursed at, and hung up on by callers. I know what it is to watch the evening news anchor passing judgment on the one time that one dispatcher got it wrong . . . and never mentioning the hundreds, the thousands of times we all got it right. I know what it is to be underpaid, overworked, understaffed, overstressed.

I don't ask to be appreciated in any great way. I just want to do my job, like anyone else. But a little understanding would mean so much.

I am proud. But I am only human.

I want to help.

I want to help you.

I am a 911 dispatcher.

We imagined this heartfelt tribute would inspire dispatch center managers to share it with their dispatchers, and with other managers so those other managers could share it with their own teams. We imagined it being printed out, framed, given as a gift, circulated in an email, included in a newsletter.

We hoped it would let our client's customers know just how much they cared.

We took this tribute, made it even more share-worthy by putting the text on a dramatic background image of a dispatcher, added a mention of our client to the bottom as the source, and posted it on our client's blog. Then we shared the link across social media. Dispatchers instantly latched on to it, sharing it over and over again, on Facebook dispatcher pages, with friends who were dispatchers, on their own pages. At one point, it became a victim of its own success—a competitor actually copied and pasted the text of the tribute without giving credit to our client as the source and shared it with their audience! And as if that weren't bad enough, it immediately began going viral on the competitor's Facebook page, as well! We acted quickly to rectify the situation, insisting that the competitor give credit where credit was due, and soon the campaign was back on track, with our client firmly in the spotlight.

To this day, that blog post is the most popular one on our client's site—and it's been quite some time since we ran that campaign! It just goes to show that a focus on the customer really does create incredible marketing momentum.

» Your Turn

So how can your company's marketing harness that same momentum by becoming more customer-focused?

It all starts with the customer personas. Who are your versions of Marketade's Annie and Bryan? You already created a more basic form of your personas in the last chapter, as you worked to lay the groundwork for agility. Now follow these steps to create your company's in-depth customer profiles, and take the first step towards a new customer focus:

1. Develop your questions.

The areas you'll need to focus on in your customer personas will vary based on whether your company is B2C (business-to-customer) or B2B (business-to-business). While a B2C marketer will want to know things about their customers' personal interests and families, a B2B marketer should focus more on job descriptions and business goals. So come up with a list of questions you want answered, in order to have the most comprehensive, 360-degree understanding of your customer persona possible.

For B2C, that might look something like this:

- What are my customers' basic demographics? Age, gender, marital status, children, occupation, income, education, location?
- What are my customers' personal interests, hobbies, passions, goals, and values?
- What is a day in the life of my customers like?
- Who are my customers' friends? How do they interact— online and in person?
- What are my customers' needs, problems, and pain points? What do they need help with?
- What image do my customers want to convey to others about themselves?

- Where do my customers hang out online, and what do they do there?
- Which blogs and websites do my customers visit?
- What are some obstacles that might prevent my customers from buying?
- What are my customers' expectations when it comes to brand experience?

For B2B, the list would, after the first question, look a bit different:

- What are my customers' basic demographics? Age, gender, occupation, industry, experience, company size, income, education, location?
- What are my customers' job descriptions, responsibilities in their places of work, and professional goals and values? What are their biggest challenges, and how do they overcome them?
- What are my customers' companies' goals? How are my customers involved in helping them reach those goals?
- What is a day in the life of my customer like? What does success look like to them?
- What tools do my customers use? What skills do they require?
- Who are my customers' colleagues, supervisors, subordinates? What are these relationships like? How does my customer go about keeping them all happy?
- What are my customers' business needs, problems, and pain points? What do they need help with? What would

make them look better to their boss? What would make life easier for them?

- Where do my customers hang out online in a professional capacity, and what do they do there?
- Which industry sites and blogs do my customers follow?
- What are some obstacles that might prevent my customers from buying?
- What are my customers' expectations when it comes to brand experience?

Add more questions as needed to tailor the information to your company. These questions will guide all the research you do and inform the personas you create, so be sure to spend ample time making them comprehensive.

2. Do your research.

The next step is to take your list of questions and start answering them, based on data you already have. Notice I said based on *data*—not on intuition or opinion or hopes or guesses or preconceived notions. And be sure the data you use isn't outdated. Access the customer data you have stored in the marketing automation software we discussed in the last chapter. Check Google Analytics, peek into the analytics of your social media accounts, look at the customer data you've already collected through any other medium. Fill in as much of the information as you can with your existing data.

3. Gather more data—by asking for it.

At this point, you're sure to have questions that still need answering. The solution? Ask your current customers! Interview them on the phone or via email. Send out surveys via email, and offer an incentive for answering. Put a form on your website to capture more detailed information. And don't forget to talk to your sales team, if you have one—they often have insight into customer trends that others in your company may miss.

4. Spend time listening on social media.

The gaps in your understanding of your customers are getting smaller, and now it's just a matter of getting those last details. Go where your customers (and others who fit the same profile) are online, and just listen. Which social media platforms do they prefer? Facebook? LinkedIn? Pinterest? Which social media groups do they belong to and actively participate in? Google+ communities? LinkedIn Groups? Listen in on those conversations. What types of content are they sharing and discussing? Which blogs do they recommend—or even write themselves? Which influencers drive thought in their circles? This information can be some of the most important in your marketing strategy.

5. Create your personas and their stories.

Finally! It's time to put it all together. Choose a name, pick a photo to go with it, and then write up your customer persona's story—the sum total of everything you've learned, put into story form, as if it was background information about one actual individual. Don't be surprised if you end up with two, three, or even more different personas—as long as they can each be clearly defined through a unique story.

6. Test your assumptions.

If you were paying attention in the last chapter, you'll know you aren't done yet. Testing and tweaking is just as vital here as it is in any other aspect of new paradigm marketing. Appeal directly to the customer segments described by your target personas. Try out a few of the marketing tactics you imagine will work well with them. Then take a look at the data, analyze the

A COMPANY GETTING IT RIGHT

The global software company SAP, mentioned in the previous chapter, is engaged in customer-centric marketing by making use of customer testimonials in its webinar campaigns. In a campaign based around a new memory technology, SAP HANA, they featured that product's customers in webcasts where they would share their experience with the product and explain how the product eases tech pain points. The company even allowed viewers to directly ask the customer presenters questions about the product during the webcasts. As Scott Feldman, Global Head of the SAP HANA Customer Community, SAP, explained, "An intelligent campaign [that involves] hear[ing] the story about your solutions and how they're impacting customers—but hearing that story directly from the customer and not the vendor—really resonates with other customers."

A key lesson here is that even B2B prospects want to hear more than just marketing messages, and that third-party validation—such as customer testimonials in this case, or opinions from thought leaders in the overall marketplace that emphasize the value of your offering—is a powerful way to influence your audience. When your messaging features independent, third-party resources—and prospects trust what those resources have to say—prospects are more likely to trust your overall marketing messaging.

response, tweak your personas or your approach to marketing to them, and try again. Soon you'll have a detailed, increasingly accurate understanding of exactly who your customers are and how best to approach them.

» Customer Focus Tools

The best way to gather information on what your customers are doing and saying online, in order to build those customer personas, is by monitoring their social media activity. One way to do this is to search on those social media platforms for mentions of your company's name—who else would be talking about you, other than your customers or your potential customers?

There are many, many social listening tools out there, but these are a few of my favorites:

- **Hootsuite and TweetDeck:** Both of these tools allow you to search Twitter in real time, looking for posts that include your company's name, even if they don't tag you or use your hashtag.
- **Social Mention:** This tool gathers data on mentions of your company name from multiple social media platforms—Facebook, YouTube, Twitter, etc.—and then lets you know whether overall sentiment towards your company is positive or negative.
- **Topsy:** This tool gathers similar data as Social Mention, but from both social media and blogs.
- **IceRocket:** This tool focuses mainly on mentions in blogs, but can also check image sites such as Flickr.
- **Google Alerts:** While this tool won't scan social media for you, it will let you know whenever your company's name is mentioned on any other website.

» Customer Focus Tips

With your data-driven customer personas in hand, you're now ready to start creating marketing strategies and campaigns based on them. That's an important first step—but that's not all there is to customer-focused marketing.

Every single action you take should be centered around the customer you are looking to attract and retain. Here are some tips to making your marketing revolve around the customer:

1. Create every marketing strategy by first putting yourself in your customers' shoes.

Don't just look from the outside when coming up with ideas—put yourself inside each of your customer personas. Imagine that you were a mom into fitness but on a budget. What kind of marketing content would catch your eye? What would convince you to spend your money? Don't make the mistake of "telling" your personas what they should be interested in. Look at the world through their eyes to find out, instead.

2. Make it all about them.

Your entire focus in marketing should be not on marketing your company to your customers, but on giving your customers the spotlight via your company. How can you make your customers the stars of your marketing campaigns? Tap into their interests and desires to find the right approach, and then take a backseat while you let them shine.

3. Let customers know about your shared values.

Customers love companies that support a cause. But they especially love companies that support a cause near and dear to *their* hearts. And when a customer buys one of your products, the one they choose gives you a good idea of where exactly their interests lie. While it's certainly praiseworthy to support your own personal charity of choice, just imagine how much your efforts can be amplified if you chose a charity that aligned with your customers' values, as well. For example, if your company sells business software, lend your support to a cause relevant to your businesspeople customers—a program training disadvantaged youth to become business leaders, for example.

If donating to charity isn't possible, share your company's *raison d'être* with your customers—if it's heartfelt, it will resonate. Maybe your gym was started because your CEO is devoted to health and fitness, or maybe you became an educational software designer because you're passionate about educating young children. Anyone buying your products or services is obviously also interested in the same thing, and will appreciate your passion for something they see as important, too.

Make your values a major part of your branding, so people associate them with your company automatically. That way, your customers will be proud to let others know that they do business with you.

4. Have conversations, don't recite monologues.

Customers today want to be a part of the action, to actively build two-way relationships with brands, rather than passively being talked at. A social media post aimed at a general audience and not giving any reason to engage will be ignored. A post aimed at a specific persona and asking for feedback or opinions or some other form of dialogue will make customers feel valued and attract engagement.

5. Provide amazing customer service.

Don't think marketing and customer service belong in the same conversation? Think again. Social media, one of your chief marketing tools, is also one of the first places customers turn to express frustration, share their appreciation, or even ask a company for help. Answering customer questions and responding to comments both positive and negative will go a long way towards letting all your customers know that you take their concerns seriously.

6. Never stop asking how you can help.

Customers' needs and preferences change over time, so assuming they'll want to receive that same email newsletter a year from now, or that Facebook will still be their favorite place to hang out online in two years, can lead to problems. If you don't adapt your strategy to fit your customers' current situation, you will lose them. To prevent this from happening, keep asking questions. Include a question in every marketing email asking whether they'd like to change the types of emails they receive from you. Watch your analytics carefully to see whether your target audience has shifted and now follows links to your site from Pinterest more often than from Facebook. Ask customers outright whether their needs have changed.

Gathering this kind of data will keep your finger on the pulse of your target audience. Not only will this let your customers see that you truly care about their preferences, but it will also enable you to make continual changes so your marketing strategy grows more and more effective.

7. Make friends with their friends.

Have you ever heard of the psychological principle called *triadic closure*? It says that two people are more likely to be closer friends if they both share a third friend in common. People like closing gaps in their social networks, and having a third friend in common gives them even more reason to trust each other. How can you use this principle to your advantage?

Connect with an influencer.

Choose a well-known figure in your industry and develop a relationship with them. It might start out with some social media banter, then morph into a guest blogging opportunity, and finally evolve into a joint webinar. Or you might just agree to promote each other's products in your own emails or social media posts.

Whatever course your friendship takes, it will benefit you both. Why? Because people in your audience who already liked that influencer will now like you even more, knowing that you two are connected—and vice versa.

8. Create content for customers' every need.

Customers today want to educate themselves fully about a product or service online before they begin talking to a salesperson or set foot in a store. As they research and come closer and closer to a decision, they move through the various stages of the sales funnel, evolving from casual visitors to committed customers. Create content for people who are just looking for basic information, as well as for those who are interested in more in-depth explanations, comparisons, and case studies. If you become the resource they turn to again and again at every stage of their journey, your company will be top of mind—and will have inspired confidence and trust as an industry expert— when they make their final decision.

9. Make that content easy to read and remember.

The human brain is hardwired to respond to stories. Researchers have found that when you're listening to a particularly boring class lecture, or reading a list of bullet points in a blog, the only parts of your brain that are activated are the language processing centers. That's it.

But when you listen to a story, suddenly a bunch of other parts of your brain get involved, too. If the story has action, your brain's motor cortex lights up. If the story describes the way something looks or smells or feels, your brain's sensory cortex lights up.

Scientists actually did an experiment where they monitored the brain of a person telling a story along with the brains of the people listening to that story. And what they found out was amazing: The storyteller was able to synchronize her audience's brain waves with her own. When the emotional center in her brain was activated by a part of her story—so were her listeners'! The same was true for *all* of her brain's activity. She was basically able to transfer her thoughts and feelings into their heads, just by telling them a story.

You can use the way people respond to stories to help you in your business. The stories we remember most are the ones that make us feel a strong emotion. Maybe they make us laugh. Maybe they terrify us. Maybe they make us feel outraged, or hopeful, or excited. In using a compelling story as part of your marketing, it doesn't matter which emotion you tap into—just as long as you tap into one.

Most important, *make your customers the heroes of the story.* Sure, they'd rather hear about how your business can help them than about how great your product or service is—benefits rather than features. But they'd rather hear *even more* about

---

>> **A COMPANY GETTING IT RIGHT**

Fiskars, a scissor company with a more than 360-year history, conducted some research and found that scrapbookers, one of their largest customer demographics, didn't really care about specific tool brands, but were very passionate about expressing their interest in their scrapbooking hobby online. To tap into this user interest, the brand reached out to scrapbook influencers via its "Fisk-a-teer" community and campaign. This effort included going to scrapbook bloggers, asking them to show Fiskars what they did while scrapbooking and to share their life. They then actually began hiring Fisk-a-teers, who were brought into the company's headquarters to be immersed in—and get excited about—the company's scrapbooking products. Those new employees served as leaders at the Fisk-a-teer online community, answering audience questions, attending scrapbook trade shows, running live chats, and blogging. Although these paid brand advocates were employees of Fiskars, they were encouraged to cover all the various scrapbook tools they were using, Fiskars branded and not.

> Although the key goal of the campaign was simply raising brand awareness with the scrapbooking audience, the team also was able to get product development insight from Fisk-a-teer community feedback, as well as a greater understanding of what new products were most likely to be popular.

how, just by buying your product, they can be as successful as the guy in your story—or how they can avoid being as dumb as the guy in your story by giving your service a try.

When you share your message as a story, and then give your customers a way to enter your story and come out the hero, you're tapping into an age-old, primal trigger that people can't help but respond to.

Customer focus means so much more than targeting a certain demographic with your marketing, or finding out what a focus group says about your marketing tactics. It is a completely different mindset in which the customer becomes an active participant in every marketing strategy and campaign. Whether the customer's involvement happens through sharing an offer on social media or uploading pictures or videos of themselves engaging with a brand, the focus is on the customer, not the company. When marketing becomes personal, momentum is the natural result.

Chapter 3 Takeaways

» Customer focus means identifying who your customers are, listening to (and acting on) their input and feedback, personalizing their experience with your company, and being a brand whose values they want to be associated with.

» Customer personas are essential to a customer-focused marketing strategy, because they enable marketers to specialize content.

» Create your personas by compiling a list of questions to ask, gathering data to answer them, listening on social media to collect more details, and then testing your assumptions.

» Using social media listening tools can help you keep tabs on what people are saying about your company, as well as giving you valuable insight into where your customers hang out online and what they do there.

» Shared values, great customer service, solicitous questions, helpful content, two-way conversations, relationships with influencers, and stories all make for great elements of a customer-focused marketing strategy.

chapter 4

3rd Principle of Momentum:
Integration

Integration means merging your digital marketing efforts with your traditional, offline marketing strategy to create a seamless brand experience for customers, no matter where they encounter your business. The more closely integrated these two aspects of marketing are, the more friction you remove from the customer's experience, and the more momentum will result as the two feed off each other.

WHEN DIGITAL MARKETING first became popular, companies created separate positions and separate departments to handle this new frontier. And that made sense at the time—it was faster, easier, and more affordable for companies to add digital marketing campaigns as a side supplement to their existing, traditional marketing methods, than to try and overhaul their entire marketing department to incorporate this new and untested medium.

Fast-forward a couple of decades, however, and not many companies have changed their approach. Digital marketing is still primarily seen as a separate endeavor from traditional marketing, with strategies and campaigns that have little if anything to do with the initiatives undertaken on the traditional side. But those few companies who *have* taken the plunge and fully integrated their digital and traditional marketing have seen new and exciting successes, with each side building on the momentum of the other.

Before the internet, marketing communications was a simple, straightforward process: Marketers talked, through a single channel, and customers listened. Now, communication back and forth between customers and marketers happens via multiple channels simultaneously, both digital and traditional—TV, social media, email, print ads. . . . Keeping those channels siloed just doesn't make sense anymore.

This new approach to marketing is such a revolution that a new word has been coined to describe it: *digical*—a merging of the digital and the physical. Global management consulting firm Bain & Company came up with the term after their research showed that more and more companies were marrying the two—and this trend is projected to keep growing exponentially over the next few years.

While integration in and of itself is important for marketing success, it requires both customer focus and agility in order to create real momentum.

From a customer focus perspective, an integrated approach to marketing is really the only approach that makes sense. Customers expect a seamless brand experience, whether they are in a store, on a website, watching a TV commercial, or on social media, with every channel conveying the same message and the same image. Why would any company want to make their customer's experience more confusing, even jarring, than it needs to be, by allowing a disconnect between their online and offline presences?

And agility is key here because integration results in massive amounts of new data about customers, which can then be used to tweak and customize marketing strategies.

Can you see how even just these first three principles of momentum, working together, are already creating a snowball effect, each augmenting the others' effectiveness?

Now let's take a look at how our friends at Marketade approach digical marketing.

» Integration in Action

Marketade's first digical campaign, the free drink offer appearing on a customer's fitness band at the end of their jogging route, was a roaring success. Combining the real-world elements of the jogging route and the stores nearby with the digital aspect of social media and connected devices made for the perfect campaign.

It was so successful, in fact, that Savanna and Stan decided to try to re-create the same magic with a new campaign. This time, they wanted to make a huge splash, so they developed an idea for a digical event launching their latest flavor.

Because their traditional and digital marketing teams were integrated, they were easily able to coordinate and come up with a strategy to make the real-world event a digital one, as well. In order to cater to their customers' passion for fitness, they decided to host a unique fitness conference complete with inspirational talks from key voices in the fitness industry, educational seminars aimed at coaches and trainers, and fun sports competitions for attendees. The event would solidify the Marketade brand as a leader in the industry.

The integration of digital and traditional began early. Teaser promotions were run on social media, letting fans and followers know that something big was in the works. The labels on Marketade bottles were changed to include cryptic references to the event, sending people to their Facebook page to find out more. Short videos on Facebook gave viewers behind-the-scenes glimpses of Marketade team members working on this mysterious project. Emails were sent out with countdowns to the day the secret would be unveiled. The excitement and anticipation built.

Finally, the day of the announcement arrived. A new website had been created specifically for the conference, and all online and offline marketing pointed traffic there to get information and register to attend. Customers were updated via social media and emails, which shared details about who would be speaking, what attendees would learn, and how much fun it would be. All posts related to the event used the same hashtag, to ensure that each one was findable by people interested in the conference.

Store displays were created to let customers know about the event, as well, and to share details about a free ticket giveaway to five lucky people. Customers could enter by visiting the Marketade Facebook page and filling out a short form.

When the big day arrived, the physical venue of the conference was saturated with reminders to go online. Attendees were encouraged to live-tweet from the event using its hashtag.

Speakers asked their audiences to ask them questions on social media in real-time during their talks. Every single piece of marketing collateral at the event from Marketade included their website and social media URLs, as well as a QR code leading to an event-specific landing page.

At the same time, Marketade's conference website live-streamed every speech, seminar, and game at the physical event. Its social media pages provided a running commentary on the events of the day, and emails went out with key speakers' presentation notes or PowerPoint slides.

By the end of the day, Marketade had utilized its integrated, digical approach to reach a vast audience, sharing a physical event with its online audience, and an online event with its physical audience. The momentum of each drove that of the other, so that the event was a smashing hit both online and offline. Due to the immersive experience, every single person who engaged with Marketade that day, whether via the internet or in person, felt he or she had created a more meaningful relationship with the company.

A COMPANY GETTING IT RIGHT

One year at Dreamforce, a huge cloud-technology conference put on by cloud computing company Salesforce, the cloud-based marketing automation software company HubSpot decided to become a platinum sponsor. Instead of the single large booth that came with that level of sponsorship, HubSpot chose to create four "un-booths" throughout the many Dreamforce venues to create the appearance of being everywhere at the event. Those areas featured HubSpot team members—in orange tracksuits to help them stand out—giving away stuffed unicorns to attendees. The stuffed animals were wearing orange capes with HubSpot's Dreamforce URL and a QR code that led to a free e-book; the event's swag bag also contained a set of rainbow unicorn stickers from HubSpot featuring the same URL and code. By the end of the event, this unique digical approach generated 2,300 leads for HubSpot.

» Integration as a Way of Life

While most companies will need to go back into existing structures and strategies and revamp them in order to introduce real integration into their marketing efforts, some businesses are born integrated, combining traditional and digital marketing from the get-go, and harnessing the resulting momentum for instant growth. One such company happens to be a client of ours, who manufactures automotive maintenance fluids.

Shortly after its birth in 2002, our client company launched its first website. From then on, its founder has put both marketing approaches to work in tandem—to great effect.

"My aim in marketing, whether digital or traditional, is to create an experience for the customer," the company founder explained. "We have a partnership with NASCAR, and I see that as an opportunity for auto technicians to say *I use NASCAR products!* And anything digital is an opportunity to get engagement—for customers to have an experience with our brand online."

A laser focus on branding is what led the company's founder to combine his online and offline marketing efforts into one integrated approach. "Why not leverage both, back and forth? Our NASCAR partnership—a traditional marketing approach—meant that it made sense for us to jump into the online conversation when Team Xtreme's #44 Sprint Cup car was stolen, so we offered a reward via social media for any information leading to its recovery—a free pit pass to every remaining Sprint Cup in the 2015 season."

The key to integrating digital and traditional marketing, our client maintains, is to stay agile enough to take advantage of relevant opportunities that pop up—through both digital and physical avenues. The company's founder told us, "In one case, we saw a chance to sponsor a UFC fighter, and we were agile enough to mobilize quickly, sponsor the fighter, and then share that information on Twitter. It's all about taking what's relevant—what makes sense—and making it an exciting, integrated experience for the customer."

That's not to say that traditional and digital marketing don't each have their own unique strengths. In the opinion of the manufacturing company's founder, the traditional approach provides a company's foundation. It creates the environment and atmosphere of a business, from the name tags employees wear to the branded gifts given to visiting customers. The digital approach, on the other hand, is more dynamic: always looking not just to stay abreast of current trends, but to get *ahead* of them, and be over-the-top relevant in the industry. Both, however, are geared towards one thing: creating brand fanatics.

» Your Turn

If you are ready to take the next step and integrate your company's traditional and digital marketing, here's a guide to making the change:

1. Break the ice.

Before you do anything else, introduce your digital and traditional marketing teams to each other! Depending on the way your marketing departments were set up and run, it could very well be that they've never met! In some companies, there is even some competition between the two teams, as each strives to prove their worth to management. Whether your teams are currently acquaintances, strangers, or competitors, it's a good idea to do some team-building exercises to break the ice and get these two teams feeling comfortable with each other. Devoting time to this now will make every subsequent step easier—and produce much better results when it comes time to start collaborating in earnest.

» ABC Bakery had been in business for decades, and their traditional marketing team had been along for the entire ride. Their digital marketing team, on the other hand, was a much later addition, and had always acted separately from the older team. Unfortunately, there was definitely friction between the two groups. The traditional team felt that they did all the heavy lifting, while the digital team got all the glory, just for playing around on Facebook all day. The digital team, on the other hand, felt that the traditional team was stuck in the past, and not willing to try anything new.

ABC's CEO decided the two teams needed to get to know each other outside the charged workplace environment, so he arranged for them to take a few days for team building. They were paired up with members of the opposite team and went on scavenger hunts around town, got into mixed teams to play some silly sports, and generally just had fun getting to know each other on a personal level. By the end of it, they were all starting to gel into one cohesive team.

2. Go for easy wins.

It won't be easy, in the beginning, to convince everyone on both sides of the marketing divide that this new integrated approach will work. It may even be tricky to get buy-in from everyone in the C-suite. That's why it's important to start by going after some low-hanging fruit, to show everyone what the possibilities of this new synergy are. Have your teams work together to add just one digital element to every traditional marketing campaign currently running, and one traditional element to each digital marketing campaign in progress. Be sure to keep an eye on the analytics to see how these changes affect conversions, so that you have hard data to back up your claim that integration will achieve the results you're looking for. This is also a great first foray into working together for both marketing teams.

» Even though they were still dubious, their newfound friendships persuaded members of each of ABC Bakery's marketing team to give integration a try. Adding just one element from the other team's area of expertise couldn't be that hard, right? Several of the company's billboards were up for a change soon, so the digital marketing team asked the traditional marketing team to add the company's Twitter URL and the hashtag #HowIKnowItsABCTime to the traditional billboard design. They then began promoting the hashtag on Twitter themselves, with tweets like, "Burned the cookies again! #HowIKnowItsABCTime" and "Cake Decorating = Pinterest Fail #HowIKnowItsABCTime." They tracked analytics to see how the campaign was affected when the billboards went up.

The traditional team, in turn, asked the digital marketing team to help them promote their radio commercials online, to leverage them further. The digital team created a fun, interactive page on the bakery website where any of their radio commercials could be played, and then sent traffic there via social media.

Analytics proved that merging digital and traditional was working, and morale was boosted all around.

3. Look over existing strategies together.

In order to work well together, each team will need to fully understand where the other one is coming from, what their approach has been, what their goals were, and what they've been able to accomplish. To that end, it's a good idea for each team to present to the other its existing marketing strategies, with all the reasoning and experience behind each one, and explain their results, as well. Once each side has had a chance to present their strategy, then it's time for everyone to step back from both approaches, and put themselves in their customers' shoes. As a customer, where are the disconnects? Where do the differences in the online and offline approaches create friction, slowing down momentum? What would a customer expect in a seamless experience, and how will you need to change in order to meet those expectations? That emphasis on customer focus is vital here, in order to get the next steps right.

» Taking the next step, the two ABC Bakery marketing teams held a meeting. The traditional marketing team explained their approach, which utilized TV and radio commercials, billboards, product placement in cooking network shows, print advertising and coupons, and in-store promotions. They discussed what their years of experience had taught them was effective, and what wasn't. Their strategy was to position ABC Bakery as a down-home country bakery, and so every aspect of their marketing was geared towards that end. Food channel stars used their products in home-style, rustic settings, the voice-overs on their radio and TV commercials always had a Southern drawl, and the imagery in print ads was red-checked gingham and sweet ol' grandmas.

Then the digital marketing team took their turn, explaining what exactly they did on social media all day, what the strategy behind it was, and what the results were. They discussed their attempts to appeal to a younger audience with humor, their focus on Pinterest-worthy food images, and their blog's emphasis on the natural ingredients used.

Once each team understood the other more fully, they looked for areas of disconnect that a customer might encounter in moving from the bakery's online marketing to the bakery's traditional marketing, and vice versa. They found that the brand voice, imagery, and messaging used in each medium differed substantially—and that needed to change.

4. Set common goals.

Of course the two marketing teams will already have common goals—your company's overarching business goals. But their departmental goals probably looked different enough that you'll need to create a new set that make sense for both teams. Many of the goals may be able to remain the same, while others will need to be tweaked. But regardless of how much actually changes, the chance to come together and understand the new set of shared goals is invaluable.

» Both marketing teams at ABC Bakery wanted to increase sales. But while the traditional team was focused on the logistics of getting the message out—landing the right product placement opportunity, producing the perfect commercial, putting ads in the right newspapers and magazines—the digital team was intensely focused on the customer—what appealed to their Facebook fans, what types of blog posts people shared, which pages on their site were visited most often.

Both aspects were important, but they needed to be merged in service of a single set of goals. So the two teams hammered out a list, and didn't stop there. They used each new goal as a way to indicate how each team's efforts would support the other's. "Increase traffic to our blog" became "Increase traffic to our blog, which will support the effort to position ABC as a country bakery through the topics chosen." And "Increase awareness through billboards" became "Increase awareness of our online presence through billboards."

5. Define roles.

For teams not accustomed to working together, this step is essential. Every team member needs to understand fully what their individual role is within the department, as well as what the role of their marketing approach, traditional or digital, is in working towards their new goals. Maybe the traditional marketing team is responsible for starting real-world campaigns that drive people towards the online channels, and then the digital marketing team takes over once they hit the website or social media pages. Or maybe teams will work tightly together to integrate campaigns every single step of the way, constantly switching back and forth between digital and physical taking the lead. Regardless of what roles are decided on, everyone needs to be aware of their responsibilities within the new structure in order for a digical approach to function well.

≫ ABC Bakery decided that the traditional marketing team and digital marketing team should work hand in hand, each building off the other in order to leverage each channel most effectively. That said, they also decided that the traditional team's main role would be to send customers online, where the digital team could then analyze their behavior via analytics. In order to do all this, they would have to collaborate closely on every campaign, from brainstorming to execution.

6. Create a new strategy together.

Now that the groundwork has been laid for the new integrated team to function, the real work can begin. Team members should collaborate to create a new marketing strategy, one that takes the new common goals and the customers' perspective into account, and merges digital and physical as closely as possible. This new digical strategy will be the guiding light behind every campaign, every initiative, every plan, from now on—a completely new mindset and approach to marketing.

>> ABC Bakery's new strategy would be to modernize its image a bit in order to stay relevant, while still staying true to its country roots. To that end, the traditional marketing team's imagery would shift from down-home grandmas to artistic glamour shots of country comfort food, while the digital marketing team's approach would begin to emphasize the country aspects of the brand in its humor. With both channels synchronized, they could then begin to build on each other's momentum.

7. Create new campaigns together.

With the new strategy in place, the team can now begin to work on individual marketing campaigns. Each one should integrate digital and physical as much as possible, while keeping your company's customer personas in mind, and focus on the customers' overall brand experience by aiming to remove as much friction as possible from the customers' path to conversion.

» ABC Bakery realized its customers wanted the family feel of country life, but with all the sophistication and high standards that today's consumers demand. The first digical campaign ABC Bakery put together was a sentimental tribute to all that country life stands for, emphasizing lush images of ABC's gorgeous country-style baked goods at rustic outdoor family celebrations, gently humorous references to country living, and a focus on the natural, sustainable aspects of country food. Blog posts were written to fit the tribute, and shared across social media and email. Images were created and shared online and via TV, print ads, and billboards. In-store signage and the website were updated to reflect the new campaign, as well. Hashtags were created to promote the tribute: #IAmCountry and #TodaysCountry.

8. Execute campaigns together.

It's one thing to brainstorm and come up with ideas with a new team—and another to actually get into the trenches with them and execute those ideas. With emotions and stress levels running high, especially during the first few campaigns when things are still unfamiliar, the work of actually implementing campaigns can cause some discord. But success breeds success—every win will bring them closer together, so that the next campaign goes even more smoothly.

» While there was some friction involved when the rubber finally met the road, the ABC Bakery marketing teams pushed through the challenges and ran a successful campaign. They found their rhythm for working together, learned how to communicate effectively with each other, and discovered their sweet spot for collaborating.

9. Measure and tweak.

Don't forget everything you learned about agility in the first chapter amidst all these changes! Your traditional marketing team may not be accustomed to using analytics to the same extent as your digital marketing team, so be sure to bring them up to speed and stay on top of that data. Take advantage of every single point of momentum you notice by tweaking your campaigns, digital and physical, to focus on areas where you're experiencing successes.

» Throughout the campaign, both ABC Bakery teams kept a close eye on analytics, and made changes accordingly. When it became clear that the food images were a hit on Pinterest, they started a competition to see which customer could take the most gorgeous shot of one of their products. When blog posts about the quality of their ingredients proved to be popular, they branched out into writing similar posts and articles for influential foodie websites and print magazines. Each change brought them more success—and increased their marketing momentum exponentially.

» Integration Tools

Integrating all of your marketing channels can be a challenge, especially when it comes to measuring results from each. But luckily, there are solutions available. Whether you'd rather go it alone or get some professional help, there's a tool or expert out there to help.

- **Smart Insights:** This site offers forms and templates for creating integrated strategies, not software—the perfect solution for a true DIYer. If you already have the team and the tracking tools in place, and just need some guidance on setting out your strategy and making it easily understandable for everyone involved, let Smart Insights be your mentor.

- **SmartMPM:** Marketing performance measurement software that provides a simple way to track the results of every channel and element of integrated marketing campaigns, so that you can determine their success.

- **Visual IQ:** A software solution that focuses on attributing successes to specific marketing channels so that you can

A COMPANY GETTING IT RIGHT

Juniper Networks, a computer network security and performance company, decided to make all collateral at its first global partner conference paperless and mobile-only. The company sent out an email in advance of the event letting attendees know that all event collateral, such as the event agenda and map of the conference center, would only be available via QR code and accessible on mobile devices. Additionally, QR codes were part of presenter slide decks and placed at exhibitor booths and on kiosks at conference events such as cocktail mixers. With this initiative, Juniper Networks made a serious commitment to taking a digical approach, and attendees loved the convenience, eco-friendliness, and cool factor of the idea.

optimize your campaigns to take advantage of the channels that are proving most effective for you.

- **Integrated marketing agency:** If you don't feel you have the right team in place to go digical, or your team needs some direction, consider hiring a marketing agency that specializes in integrated marketing. Such an agency can set up your initial integrated strategy, help you run your first few campaigns, and show you how to tweak them for maximum effect.

» Integration Tips

There are myriad ways to use offline interactions with consumers to advance your online marketing, from the very simple (such as posting signs in your stores or offices to share your website and social media addresses with customers) to the more sophisticated (such as displaying a custom hashtag on the screen during a TV commercial to encourage people to engage). I've put together a list of some creative ideas to help get you started.

1. Book speaking engagements.

Any time that you or any of your employees is asked to speak at a seminar, conference, or convention—and especially if your company puts on an event itself—is a golden opportunity to merge your offline and online marketing efforts. There are an infinite number of ways to integrate social media into your talk.

A speaker can post a discussion question pertinent to his topic on Facebook or Google+, and then ask attendees to take out their smartphones and tablets and respond, right there during the talk. The web page in question can be displayed on the wall with a projector for all to see, as motivation to join in the discussion, and the speaker can reference specific people's comments while speaking, even asking them by name to wave from their seat or continue their thoughts out loud.

The speaker could also post a few of the most important takeaways on social media, and invite attendees to submit questions about the presentation on Facebook or Google+ in real-time, to be read off by the presenter, rather than the questioner having to shout them across an auditorium.

Instead of handing attendees slips of paper to rate the presentation, speakers can ask them to like the company Facebook page as a sign that they approved, or even to comment in response to a posted question such as "Did you find today's discussion of _____ to be helpful?"

Speakers can encourage attendees to sign up for their company's email newsletter, incentivizing their subscription by offering either notes summarizing the talk, a PowerPoint file of the presentation, a workbook to put into practice what was discussed, or even a secret bonus e-book or white paper exclusively for those who attended. And they shouldn't expect their audience to sign up on their own later—instead, they should walk them through the process while they're still in their seats, to ensure maximum participation.

Whenever possible throughout a presentation, get attendees liking, commenting, tweeting, following, and subscribing—in other words, engaging. While they are still in your audience, they are much more likely to engage than if you simply ask them to do it afterwards. That real-world, in-person connection makes a big difference.

2. Provide offline content.

There's nothing that a company's online audience loves to see more than a behind-the-scenes look at the inner workings of that business. Whether it's the silly antics of employees, a sneak peek at a product in development, or a few words from the CEO, consumers love to feel connected to the real people behind a business.

It may take a few extra minutes on a regular basis to capture and then publish offline content, but it's worth it for the heightened online engagement it will produce. Take pictures of employees working or goofing off, eating lunch or in training. Post them on Facebook or Instagram, asking for captions, or providing your own funny ones.

Post pictures of new job sites or new products, or short videos of the same. Even better, create short videos of various employees talking about their work. Heartfelt explanations of a company's mission, teasers for new projects in the works, and good-natured pranks or jokes all tend to be wildly popular online. Bringing some real-world experience of your company to your online audience will significantly boost their sense that they have a relationship with you.

3. Share old-fashioned notes.

Whenever anyone from your company interacts with a customer in person, in the real world, they should give that customer a printed note asking them to go online and do whatever it is you'd like them to do there, whether that's signing up for your emails, liking you on Facebook, following you on Twitter, leaving positive feedback for you on a review site, or any other goal you have.

Left to their own devices, customers just aren't as likely to post a positive review or like a company online after a good experience as they are to post a negative review after a bad one. By asking them to give a testimonial or even just to do something as simple as liking your Facebook page, and then handing them easy-to-follow instructions for exactly how to do that, they'll be much more likely to comply than if you never mentioned it.

4. Establish a local focus.

Another way to interpret the term *digical* is as the combination of digital and local. And what stronger connection to the physical is there for customers than the local? Approaching integration by focusing on the regional or local allows purely digital marketing tactics while making your marketing still seem more physical.

Something as simple as showing support for a local sports team in a social media post creates a physical connection with a location and an actual sports event in the minds of customers. If your company has a brick-and-mortar location, you can also reach out to other local businesses in blog posts and on social media to create that same connection. Write a blog post rating your favorite local spots, and then tag those businesses in your posts to let them know. Not only will you solidify your physical presence in your community, you might just gain some

A COMPANY GETTING IT RIGHT

Firefish, a small U.K.-based online recruitment software company, decided to attend industry events "virtually" rather than in person. This meant uncovering the main points of each speaker and quickly producing blog posts that addressed those points while the event was still in progress—and then sharing links to those posts on social media via the event hashtag. The approach allowed them to save its marketing budget for other channels while still taking advantage of event marketing. The CEO of Firefish said she found the approach so successful that the company has no plans to actually attend any events for the foreseeable future.

A COMPANY GETTING IT RIGHT

When international shoe company Nike was getting ready to launch its new Nike Free Run+ 3 shoe in 2012, it made it available online first, to people already registered in the NIKEiD program—a program that allowed customers to customize everything from the color to the design of their new shoes before ordering. NIKEiD participants responded by creating more than a million designs—in only two weeks. The buzz that came from this massive response created "enormous momentum and high sell-through . . . when the Nike Free Run+ 3 hit retail shelves," said company executive Christiana Shi.

extra traffic if those businesses share your post with their own audiences.

If your business is purely online, use analytics to determine where the majority of your customers live, and then do some research into local businesses in those cities. Promote those businesses in the same way, and you'll establish yourself in your customers' minds as a physical presence in spite of the fact that you're 100 percent online.

Customers today expect brands to provide a consistent, seamless experience both online and offline. The only way to deliver this is to fully integrate your digital and traditional marketing efforts. Doing so removes the friction from the customer experience, allowing momentum to build. It's not about traditional campaigns and digital campaigns anymore—it's about digical campaigns: marketing strategies that leverage the strengths of each to become more than the sum of their parts. Agility through analytics and customer focus come together via integration, enabling your company to ramp your marketing up to the next level.

Chapter 4 Takeaways

» Integration means seamlessly merging traditional and digital marketing strategies and tactics, creating a consistent brand experience for the customer.
» *Digical* refers to the integration of the digital and the physical.
» Customer focus and agility are both integral aspects of digical marketing.

» Utilize marketing performance measurement tools to ascertain which digital and physical channels are driving marketing momentum.

» Integrate digital elements into conferences, trade shows, and other real-world marketing activities, while merging offline or local elements into digital marketing efforts, in order to allow each channel's momentum to build on the other's.

chapter **5**

4th Principle of Momentum:
Content Curation

Information is common. Knowledge—information contextual-ized by wisdom—is rare. In a world filled with noise, your customers yearn for filters to help them find the signal. Curating the right content through the filter of your unique expertise, and making sure that content is also current, relevant, and easily accessible, builds your credibility with customers. Becoming the go-to resource in your industry makes your marketing momentum unstoppable.

THERE ARE HUNDREDS of websites now that let you buy or sell a house directly, thanks to today's technology. Listings online providing in-depth information about each property, allowing you to peek inside each house via pictures, and giving data about everything from mortgage payment amounts to neighborhood demographics. Through these websites, the entire transaction can occur without a middleman. Yet the majority of home buyers and sellers choose to engage an agent. Why? Because information isn't a substitute for knowledge.

While your audience may have more information than ever before today, that doesn't mean they know what to do with it. They need someone to make sense of it for them. Someone to serve as a knowledge filter. If you can take content and curate it in an intelligent way for your audience, providing them with the guidance they're searching for, you'll turn them into customers.

Does the word *curation* conjure up images of sleek art museums and state-of-the-art libraries? Curating art or litera-ture isn't as different from online content curation as you might think. Both choose the best representatives of their genre to showcase to the public. Both present material through their own unique lens. And both guide the viewer on a journey through that material, so that he or she comes out the other end with a new understanding of it.

Content marketing used to mean collecting and sharing content with an online audience. It also involved creating mas-sive amounts of your own content, hoping to stay on Google's good side through sheer volume. And in the early days of con-tent marketing, that wasn't the wrong approach—at that time, there weren't nearly as many resources available online for con-sumers as there are currently, so pushing out helpful informa-tion in large quantities drew customers easily. But with so much content now flooding the internet, businesses looking to gain marketing momentum these days know that today's curation requires a much more nuanced approach.

It's not enough to simply collect or even create content anymore. Content must be presented in an organized way, such that it is easy to navigate and easy to find. It must be kept up-to-date at all times, so that no matter when a potential customer accesses it, they will find the information relevant and helpful. It must be presented through the lens of your company's expertise and wisdom, so that customers have a reason to come to *your* site rather than the myriad of other sites with the same basic information. And every single piece of content must be of the highest quality.

Forcing website visitors to wade through an unorganized blog, outdated posts, or generic, speed-written content in order to find what they're looking for is not the way to build marketing momentum. Instead, smooth the path for your customers by making it easy for them to find the relevant, in-depth information they need, with the expert spin that only you can provide.

Remember the principle of customer focus from chapter 3? Here it is again. Effective content strategy is all about considering the experience of the customers.

So what is the best way to harness content curation to drive marketing momentum? Let's take a look at Marketade's approach.

» Curation in Action

Marketade has always been a forward-thinking company, so of course Savanna and Stan in Marketing have a content curation strategy in place. First of all, they let their brand messaging serve as the lens through which they present all of their content. Marketade is the sports drink for sports and fitness gurus, so every piece of content on their site is written from their perspective as a company well-versed in sports and fitness research, and for an audience composed of sports and fitness experts—and those who wish to become expert, as well. Because of their unique take on trending issues in the field of fitness, and their expertise in that area in general, sports and fitness enthusiasts from beginners to experts flock to their site to read what they have to say about the latest news and to get fitness information they know they can trust.

Secondly, Marketade's content is well-organized by topic. Visitors searching for information on a particular area of fitness can easily find it, simply by skimming the topic headings listed on their Resources page, rather than having to click through page after page of blog posts, or search via the site's internal search engine. That ease of navigation encourages website visitors to return to get more fitness information as needed, since they know it'll be a quick and easy visit.

Third, Marketade understands the importance of quality content. Sometimes their writers spend days writing and perfecting just one blog post. That means they can't churn out as much content as other companies—but it also means that the content they do create is 1000 percent more effective at drawing in those customers. Why? Not only does Google reward higher-quality content with better search engine results page rankings through its complex algorithms, but if the humans who read those posts feel the quality is genuinely great, they are more likely to stick around longer, return to read more regularly, and share what they read with friends. A few short paragraphs talking about generic fitness advice? No, thanks. In-depth analysis of the most cutting-edge new fitness trends, complete with interviews, stats, and embedded videos demonstrating each one? Yes, please!

But all of that is just the foundation for a great content curation strategy. Marketade also has an ongoing curation to-do list that ensures that every single piece of content they provide to customers on their site is always the best it can be, and is always being leveraged to the fullest.

Every month, Stan and Savanna go through some of the older blog posts on the site. Fitness advice changes with new research and new trends, and they don't want any potential customers finding outdated or incorrect information anywhere on their site, even if it's clearly marked with an older publish date. So they check for any posts that need to be updated, and then go ahead and make the necessary changes, adding a note to each one that it was updated on such-and-such a date, to let people know it's relevant to the state of the industry today.

In addition, they are careful to add several links in every new blog post they publish to other content on their site. Doing so helps customers find even more information on subjects they're interested in, keeps them on the website longer, and ensures that all Marketade's content, including older posts, is being utilized fully in their marketing efforts.

Finally, Marketade is constantly repurposing their content. They may take ten blog posts about nutrition and turn them into an e-book for free customer download, or take a recent webinar on the latest scientific research on sport drinks and turn it into a white paper. They sometimes make statistic-filled infographics from their blog posts, or make blog posts from podcasts of interviews they record with fitness legends. They may take days to create the perfect blog post, but then they leverage it to the fullest, presenting the material in different ways to appeal to customers' different content consumption preferences.

With their unique, quality, well-organized content, and their efforts to make the most of every piece of content ongoing, Marketade has become one of the most trusted resources in the fitness industry. And credibility equals momentum. Would you rather buy a product from a company putting out the same second-rate content as everyone else in the industry, or the company whose content is insightful and unique? That's what I thought.

» Clear Curation

Let me give you another great example of successful content curation. One client of ours is a company that designs and produces trade show booths and exhibits for other companies. To ensure that their customers have a successful trade show experience, it is in our client's best interests to educate their customers—and potential future customers—about how to make the most of every trade show. To that end, together we created an amazing online resource center where their customers can learn anything and everything about trade shows.

We helped our client wrangle their existing content—from videos to white papers to blog posts—into a manageable library of resources that customers would be able to quickly scan for the information they needed. Divided by format, and then subdivided by topic, their info center covered every aspect of trade show marketing in every possible format a customer might want to consume that content.

But we didn't stop there. Once we had the information organized, we got to work updating older content, making it relevant to today's trade show industry, as well as ensuring it conformed to current SEO standards for easier findability on Google. We completely rewrote huge numbers of outdated white papers, creating different sets of resources for businesspeople at every level of familiarity with trade shows, from complete novices to seasoned veterans. We reworked years' worth of blog posts to reflect the latest trends and posted videos of recent webinars, all to ensure the library was complete. Piece by piece, we made sure that every piece of content on their site, no matter how old, would be valuable to their customers, and so could continue to be leveraged.

We also created one page with links to more resources on other websites—curating outside content specially chosen because of its benefits to our client's customers. Presenting such a comprehensive list of additional industry resources made our client appear even more authoritative.

With all of this in place, our client's marketing momentum skyrocketed. Sharing their content via social media and email just accelerated the process, so that the work on the resource center really paid off in terms of boosted traffic and increased conversions.

» Your Turn

So how can you get started curating content for your company? Here's a step-by-step guide.

1. Thoroughly audit the content on your website.

In order to understand what you'll need to do to become an expert content curator, you first need to see where you stand. Look at everything currently on your site—blog posts, articles, e-books, white papers, videos, FAQs, even the content on each of your web pages. This won't be a quick, one-day task, so be prepared to devote some time to going in-depth here.

A COMPANY GETTING IT RIGHT

Upworthy was co-founded in 2012 by the former executive director of MoveOn.org, a nonprofit progressive policy advocacy group, and a former managing editor of *The Onion*, with a simple mission statement:

> *Upworthy draws massive amounts of attention to things that matter. Every day, our curators scour the web to find compelling, meaningful media—stories, information, videos, graphics, and ideas that reward you deeply for the time you spend with them.*

Curation is the site's chief work: finding positive video content and then putting it in a place where visitors can easily find and share that content. Upworthy is an extremely popular website, with many videos going viral. The sheer fact that they share a video *is* the commentary and filter they provide—by sharing, they are saying that a video is positive, uplifting, and worth watching.

First, note what topics you cover in your content, the formats your content is in, and how many pieces of content address each particular topic. This will be helpful for you later, in determining what content you need to add to balance out your resource offerings.

Then, take a look at the architecture of your current content. Is it all available from one central page, easily divided by topics or formats? Is it randomly spread across several different pages? Are the various pieces of content interlinked, each referring traffic to the others? Think like your customer—how easy would it be for a newcomer to your site to find relevant content?

Next, look at your content's quality. Longer is almost always better, multimedia is better than plain text, and ease of reading is vital—which means plenty of bullet points and lists and sub-headings. Perhaps most importantly of all, does your content address topics through the filter of your unique expertise? If you've basically just been rewriting generic content that's easily findable anywhere online, you're not providing your customers with value. But if you've been creating your own tips, or addressing industry trends from your own viewpoint, you're on the right track.

Finally, note which pieces of content have outdated information that needs to be updated in order for them to be relevant. If you have stats, results of studies, even commentary on older trends or news, you'll need to do the research again to see what has changed and add updates on the latest developments.

» Dr. John I. Ball, a LASIK surgeon, wanted to turn his eye care practice's website into an amazing eye health resource for his current and prospective patients. He already had a smattering of eye disease reference pages and a blog with info on the latest research and eye care tips, but he knew it wasn't set up the way it needed to be, and it definitely wasn't the highest quality content. So he performed an in-depth audit on his site. He found that he was missing key pieces of information about eye diseases and their treatments, and that the organization of his content definitely left something to be desired. He also noted that most of his blog posts were short and text-heavy; they needed to be lengthened, include more images, and be broken up visually through bullet points and subheadings. Finally, he made a note of multiple posts he needed to update with the latest research and stats.

2. Take a look at your analytics.

Which blog posts, videos, and web pages get the most traffic on your site? Which white papers and e-books get downloaded most often? There's a reason that these particular pieces of content are your most popular ones—they are the ones where you've hit the nail on the head in appealing to your customers.

Look carefully at the voice you used, the topics you chose, and the approach you took. I'm betting these posts are the ones in which you demonstrate your own unique expertise in the industry—the originality and your enthusiasm in writing or speaking about something you are passionate about shines through. Your goal will be to create more content like your most popular pieces, and to edit your older content to come as close to these pieces as possible, as well.

》 Dr. Ball looked at the analytics for his content and found that two categories of blog post and web page did particularly well with his website's visitors: eye disease information and general eye care tips. He read through his top several posts in each category, and realized these were also the posts written in the simplest language, so that anyone could understand them. That meant that the posts he had written about scientific research were going over his patients' heads. He realized he needed to go back and edit his older content to make it more understandable, and moving forward, write more about topics similar to the ones that did well, using simple language to explain them.

3. Decide on your unique content filter or lens.

Of course you already know what your brand's messaging is, and where exactly your company's expertise lies. All you have to do is find a way to apply that to your content. Will your content be written in the voice of an individual, giving a unique personal take on industry matters and dispensing advice gained from years of experience? Or will your content come from your company as an experienced, expert team? How will you comment on industry trends? How will you put your own unique spin on tips and advice? How can you stamp every single piece of content with something that makes it unmistakably yours? Be sure that whatever you decide on, it meshes with what you've discovered appeals to your audience through analytics.

》 Dr. Ball decided to brand himself as the eye doctor who explained things like complex eye conditions, scientific research, and complicated treatments in such a way that anyone could understand. This would let him build on the momentum he had already discovered in that area through looking at his analytics.

4. Determine the new structure of your resource center.

As the leader in your field, educating your audience through content, you have to consider more than just what you write and how you write it—you also need to think about how you present that content to your customers. Even if you have, hands-down, the best content in your industry, if it's confusing to get to or difficult to find, you won't gain any benefits from it—and neither will your customers.

That's why it's important to create some sort of organized resource center on your website, from which all of your content can be easily accessed. Maybe it's simply a drop-down menu on your navigation bar listing all the topics visitors can find information on. Or maybe it's a dedicated web page with links to and descriptions of each subpage. The key is to keep your organizational scheme clean and simple and easy to understand at a glance.

Next comes the tricky part. As the go-to resource for your customer, it's your job to guide visitors through your content with purpose. Simply listing topics at random and then placing related content in each category doesn't cut it. Instead, think about the journey you want your customer to take. Where should they start? Where should they finish? Consider the sales funnel, as well as the differing needs of newcomers to the industry versus old hands. Would it make more sense for a visitor to start out by watching a video, then dive into blog posts, and eventually end up reading white papers? Or maybe it would be a good idea to start out with beginner-level material across formats, and then progress into more complex discussions as he or she learns more. Lead customers through your content in a way that makes sense—this is as important to your unique content lens as the way you actually write the material.

» In keeping with his brand, Dr. Ball wanted his resource center to be as clear and well-organized as possible. Thinking about it from the perspective of a patient, he divided content into sections for eye diseases and their treatments, general eye care tips, LASIK information, new research, and other relevant categories. That way, patients could easily find what they needed at a glance.

5. Find your audience's content preferences, and aim to please.

Using your customer personas, as well as your analytics, find out what sort of content add-ons or upgrades appeal to your particular audience. Do they prefer blog posts with embedded videos? White papers with numerous statistics? Long articles with screenshots and graphs and other images illustrating points? Whatever it is they like, give them more of it by making it a point to include those extras in every single piece of content you create. If images make a difference in your traffic and the time they spend on your pages, then spruce up all your content, old and new, with more images. If videos are the thing, include one—or more—in every post. If in-depth research really gets your customers going, do more of it. Find out what your winning tactic is, and use it to the fullest.

>> Dr. Ball knew that images were a great way to illustrate concepts even more clearly than words, so he decided to start including at least three images in each piece of new content, and to go back and add images to old content, as well. He also decided to create two to three infographics a month for his site, since they too are a great way to explain concepts through images.

6. Decide how to incorporate outside content.

Curating outside content—collecting and sharing content from other companies, groups, and even individuals—can be an important part of a complete content curation strategy, as well. The key is deciding how best to incorporate it into the mix. Will you create a web page with a list of outside resources? Regularly write blog post round-ups of the best content from around the web? Link to outside content in your own blog posts? Share resources via social media posts? Decide on a plan for how and where to incorporate that outside content, and then don't forget to add your own commentary to remain consistent with the content lens you're using for everything else.

>> Dr. Ball decided to create an entire web page dedicated to more helpful eye care resources for his patients. He posted a list of links to every major eye health organization in the U.S. and the world, along with links to trusted eye care websites. Under each link, he wrote up his own opinion of the content on that site, in order to filter it through the lens of his branding.

He also decided to take a unique tack in sharing links to articles via social media. Instead of simply sharing links to something that might be over his average patient's head, he would share a link and then follow that up by sharing links to blog posts of his own, in which he would write simpler explanations of the information in the link, in order to strengthen his brand position.

7. Work on that content!

Now that you have all the pieces in place, get going with the work of actually updating and beefing up your content, restructuring your resource center, and creating higher-quality new content. Don't expect it to be done in a day, a week, or even a month—a thorough overhaul of your content may very well take several months, but it's worth it.

Update your content with the latest in SEO standards, industry information, and your unique content lens. Make it longer and easier to read. Add videos and images. Make it more similar to your most popular content.

As you finish updating each piece, begin linking to it—not just in your newly organized resource center, but in your new content, as well as in your old. Promote certain pieces of your content within other pieces of your content. Reference a relevant blog post in your e-book, or tell viewers of a video to download your white paper on a related subject. Make every effort to saturate your customers with the information they need, making it as easy as possible to access.

» Dr. Ball got to work updating all his older content, filling in the blanks where needed and boosting quality as necessary. He added images, replaced outdated stats with the most current information, and added a few more paragraphs to each piece of content to beef it up. He added links to other posts in every piece, so that someone interested in a given topic would easily be able to click from post to post learning more. Finally, he created his new resource center—organized in a clear, intuitive way, comprehensive in what it covered, and full of high-quality content that explained difficult subjects in easy to understand language. Now patients would be able to easily find anything they needed, understand what was said, and even enjoy the experience!

8. Decide how you'll repurpose your content.

Once you have your existing content optimized, it's time to use it to create more new content to leverage. (It's much quicker and easier than just writing more!) Take those seminars and make them into blog posts. Create a slideshare out of an infographic. Bundle blog posts into e-books, or deconstruct a white paper to make several articles. Come up with a game plan for repurposing every single thing you write—and not just in one way, but in two or three different ways each. That way you'll always have plenty of fresh, original content to share with your customers, working to establish you as a leader in your field.

» To pursue his goal of educating patients even further, Dr. Ball decided to create a series of e-books discussing various aspects of eye health. Not having the time to sit down and write them all out at once, however, he resolved to write them first as a series of blog posts over a few months, and then to simply bundle those posts into e-books.

He also came up with an idea to make LASIK surgery less intimidating for patients—creating videos of himself performing the procedure and then interviewing the patients afterward. The use of video fit his goal of ensuring his explanations were easy to understand and gave him even more material to use for blog posts—case studies, as it were. His idea was a hit, and patients began flocking to his site for information.

» Curation Tools

It's one thing to curate your own content, and quite another to find outside content that is insightful and relevant enough to add to your collection online. Once you find the right content to share, there's also the matter of actually sharing it—adding commentary, posting to each social media channel, spacing posts out for optimal timing. . . . The time and effort it takes can be daunting—unless you use one of these tools to help.

- **Scoop.it:** Allows you to find content easily through "smart searches," then add your own spin to it and share it with your customers.
- **Feedly:** Creates a personalized newsfeed for you, based on categories you select, so that you always have access to the latest news and conversations in your industry.
- **Curata:** Another tool that gathers content for you—but its focus is much more on data and analytics in the world of content marketing and content curation than any of the other tools listed.
- **Storify:** Lets users access social media posts from around the web, and then merge them into a story or timeline tracing a conversation or trending news.

- **Sniply:** A link-shortening tool with a twist—when you use it to share links to outside content via social media, it allows you to add a call to action to drive traffic back to your website.
- **Trapit:** Finds content for employees to share with their own social networks on behalf of their company, in order to expand the reach of the company's thought leadership to their personal networks.

» Curation Tips

Looking for some ideas on how to implement your content curation strategy? Give these tips a try.

1. Take advantage of third-party research in your content.

Find third-party research that's relevant to your messaging, and make it available to your audience to help support the conversation you are already having with them. There's a wealth of research being published on a regular basis: industry statistics, surveys of industry leaders and brand-side marketers, general insights, and more. Some of the larger independent sources for research include Gartner Inc., Forrester Research, and McKinsey & Company. And many industry vendors and agencies have research arms that produce independent research that you can cite.

Combining a number of different resources to help bolster your message gains you credibility—and sharing third-party validation of your points supports the idea of your site as a go-to destination for your audience. Of course, while providing this third-party research you should still make sure and add your own commentary to offer additional insights for your audience, in order to present that information through your own filter of expertise.

2. Tap into influencers and other subject matter experts.

Another way to add third-party credibility to your content mix is reach out to influencers and subject matter experts for insights to include in your content. To really maximize the curation impact, allow these influencers and experts to include their own suggestions on additional material your audience might find interesting. This helps expand the types of content

> ### A COMPANY GETTING IT RIGHT
>
> Analytic software company Actuate runs a large number of webinars, as many as six per month. An important aspect of their content marketing strategy was creating a content library of its webinar replays to make it easy for website visitors to find the webinar that they wanted to watch. Actuate's library was segmented by product lines, so when the marketing team would send emails around a specific product, they could easily include a link to the relevant webinar replays.
>
> Organizing its webinar content in the library provided Actuate's web visitors value, and also made the marketing team's job easier. In this case, curation took the form of organizing content in a logical way, for the benefit of customer and company alike.

that you're offering your audience and supplies them with valuable content that you might not have thought of.

Allowing third-party experts to directly address your audience builds your credibility because you're demonstrating that you aren't just pushing your message out over and over again, but you are using your marketing platform to expand the resources that your customer, by engaging with you, has available.

Don't forget about internal subject matter experts! Every company has experts such as engineers and developers who might rarely be heard from, but whose insights also provide credibility, because those messages are coming from a source outside of Marketing or Sales. One way you can make use of your internal experts is to allow your audience to ask them questions directly. Their ideas will likely be different than those of more marketing- or media-driven influencers and outside experts, since their area of expertise lies elsewhere, and they are uniquely qualified to answer questions that center around your actual products and services.

3. Make your audience part of the process.

Your audience can and should be involved in the curation process, as well. This can be as simple as just adding a call-to-action at the bottom of blog posts asking for your audience to comment with their thoughts and ideas on what you've presented. In doing so, you are once again turning part of your content over to a third party, whose input provides a completely different perspective. In the process you'll forge a bond between your company and its audience that might not materialize through sharing company and influencer content alone. For this type of audience input, you can do a certain amount of moderating to avoid anything overly negative about your brand, but generally you want to allow the conversation to remain open and at least somewhat free-wheeling; your readers will take the conversation in whatever direction they feel is most useful.

Another way that you can inject your audience into the conversation is by collecting and sharing comments and reviews from customers. In the case of comments sent via email or an online form, make sure the person sharing with you understands that you might be using their input in your content marketing. For reviews, be sure to keep editing to a minimum. A string of nothing but glowing reviews can look untrustworthy, and customers notice when negative comments are deleted, so allowing comments to stand as written, even if they contain complaints or concerns, is important. Rather than editing or deleting, write a prompt response to negative reviews addressing the issue.

4. Share lists of relevant links.

Whether you use a content curation tool or find links to outside content yourself, regularly share links that you think your audience will find valuable. This can be done in a number of ways, including:

- In blog posts about specific topics that share links and recap their content
- Via social media such as Twitter tweets or Facebook posts

- In email newsletters that offer recipients outside links that grabbed your attention plus related links to your own content

A COMPANY GETTING IT RIGHT

You know Pinterest as social media marketing platform, but it's also a place where users (including marketers and brands) create boards of curated content. That means that looking at Pinterest's popularity is a good way to see how effective content curation can be. According to research from GlobalWebIndex, Pinterest's active users grew 97 percent from the first quarter of 2014 to the first quarter of 2015, the largest growth of any social media platform, and its 70 million and counting users are sharing content at amazing rates. And they're doing more than just sharing—88 percent of those users are purchasing products that they've curated on the platform through "Pins" on their online boards. Clearly people are drawn to being able to curate content, and they are just as clearly drawn to looking at curated content—even when the curation is as simple as a group of links and images on a board with no more filter than its title.

Not only does this give you credibility as a curator of information your audience wants to find, but especially in email newsletters, it also helps offset promotional messages, letting your audience know that your marketing messaging is about helping them rather than about pushing your message at them over and over again and pressing them for a purchase. For social media, follow a rule of thumb—maybe 80 percent to 20 percent or two-thirds to one-third—as a ratio for informational versus promotional messaging, and then split that larger information percentage in half between sharing your own content and sharing other content that your audience will find useful.

Content curation is all about leveraging content in every way possible. In many ways, less is more. That is, you can create less new content (although you don't want to stop creating new content, by any means!) and actually improve your content marketing results. The key is to put the *right* content in front of your audience, not the most content.

Chapter 5 Takeaways

» Content curation means presenting content through the filter of your unique expertise, and making sure that all of it is current, relevant, high quality, and easily accessible.

» Curating content allows businesses to take fuller advantage of the marketing momentum found in their most popular pieces of content.

» In the world of content curation, quality trumps quantity.

» Multiple tools exist to help locate, leverage, and share relevant content from across the web.

» Include third-party research, influencers, and even your audience in your content strategy to gain credibility.

chapter **6**

5th Principle of Momentum:
Cross-Pollination

>>> **Cross-pollination** means incorporating every single resource your company has into your marketing strategy, allowing each to inform your use of the others. With each one of these typically untapped resources contributing to the mix, you create something new and powerful from the synergy, and your marketing momentum grows dramatically as a result.

W HY ARE BEES so important? It's not because of their honey. It's because, as they fly from flower to flower, they spread tiny amounts of pollen. This process, pollination, dramatically increases the amount of food plants produce.

Cross-pollination describes what occurs when pollen from one plant is spread to another plant. And when pollen from two different plants mix, it can end up producing something unique and new.

Cross-pollination in marketing—incorporating every single resource your company has into your marketing strategy, allowing each to inform your use of the others—has these same beneficial effects. When you leverage all of your company's resources, integrating them into your marketing strategy, not only will you end up with something unique, new, and exciting—you'll also experience exponentially more marketing momentum.

We've already talked about integration in this book; cross-pollination is something different. Where integration calls for bringing together digital and traditional marketing resources in order to offer customers one cohesive, seamless brand experience and thus exponentially magnify its effectiveness, this fifth and final principle of marketing momentum extends even further, demanding that *every* available resource be drafted into the service of marketing. This can mean leveraging your employees (company-wide—not just those in marketing!), or your strategic partners, or even outside vendors. Every relationship, every connection, has the potential to boost your marketing momentum.

This mindset is radically different from the traditional one, in which separation reigns: online from offline, marketing-related from non-marketing-related. It's an approach that is meant to, as I like to say, squeeze every last drop of juice out of the orange—to get every possible marketing benefit from any and all business resources available.

Of course, our friends at Marketade have been cross-pollinating for a while now—let's take a peek at how they've made it a part of their marketing strategy.

» Cross-Pollination in Action

Savanna and Stan are experts in marketing. But they never claimed to be experts in the science of fitness. Sure, they know enough to promote Marketade to fitness fanatics, but no more than that. So Stan and Savanna are aware that, in order to demonstrate Marketade's fitness expertise to customers and market their product as the drink of fitness gurus, they have to take advantage of existing relationships with actual fitness experts.

How do they do this? First of all, they look within their own company. Their sports drink was, after all, developed by a team of researchers who were expert in the field of fitness hydration. So they utilize that resource to the fullest, interviewing the researchers about the science behind the products for blog posts and podcasts, asking them to write up articles to use as public relations pieces on major industry websites, and even getting their input on which aspects of the drink to focus on in their marketing. Pollinating their marketing content with the expert information from these researchers boosts its effectiveness significantly among Marketade's target audience.

Secondly, they leverage existing relationships with their partners. Since Marketade is sold in health food stores and gyms, Stan and Savanna make sure to work closely with these retailers on marketing that benefits both parties. If a health food store partner is having a storewide 10-percent off sale, you can bet that Marketade will be promoting it on their Facebook page or via an email to their subscriber list, and then adding a pitch for their own products. Stan and Savanna also worked to make deals with those same retailers so that they would mention Marketade promotions in their emails and social media posts, too. If a gym partner is running a membership special, Marketade is there, too, offering an online coupon for a free sports drink to all new members—which is advertised as one of the perks of membership on the gym's website. Each marketing effort builds on the momentum of the others, and all partners enjoy a boost from the collaborative marketing efforts.

Third, Stan and Savanna also work to create relationships with outside industry experts—influencers within the industry—and then use those to their marketing advantage, as well. They reach out to fitness gurus with large followings online, asking if they would like to receive free samples of their sports drink to review on their sites, or whether they would be willing to allow Marketade to guest blog for them. When an influencer agrees, his or her existing marketing momentum instantly transfers to Marketade, as a new audience is exposed to Marketade's message.

The Marketade team also uses cross-pollination by leveraging even their outside vendors, such as their design agency and their promotional items company, in their marketing efforts. Every week, Stan and Savanna distribute sample tweets and Facebook posts to team members of every vendor they use, as well as to their own internal team members. These pre-made social media posts are designed to give team members an easy way to help Marketade promote its brand and products among their own personal social networks. In order to make sharing these posts more attractive, each week someone is picked to win a fun token prize based on a new set of criteria aimed at encouraging attractive marketing content—funniest tweet about Marketade, cutest image with Marketade, etc. Vendors and team members are encouraged to tag Marketade in their posts, to make sure Stan or Savanna sees them. This almost grassroots approach builds momentum from the bottom up, rather than from the top down.

By tapping into these usually untapped resources, Marketade created new and exciting marketing campaigns that would otherwise not have existed. Building on the momentum of multiple, cross-pollinated resources, these initiatives couldn't help but boost Marketade's momentum dramatically.

» Fruitful Cross-Pollination

A real-world example of cross-pollination comes from Haggar, the clothing manufacturer—a Marketing Zen client.

Haggar, a company with a long history and a proud tradition of quality, wanted to make sure that its digital presence reflected its strong position in the marketplace and its decades of history, while at the same time being accessible and engaging to a new generation. They had no social presence when we began work together, and we had to find a way to quickly translate their traditional following onto digital channels. We looked at their existing offline relationships and found that while Haggar didn't have a social following yet, retailers they worked with, such as JCPenney and Kohl's, had established social media channels. We reached out to those retailers and asked if they would be interested in cross-promoting. They were thrilled. Not many manufacturers had really engaged them in this way before, and they saw the mutually beneficial opportunity it presented. By working with those retailers in an ongoing fashion, often tagging them in Haggar social media posts, we broadened Haggar's reach to include their partners' online audiences, as well. These cross-promotional efforts also boosted Haggar's credibility among multiple demographics, by associating them with major retailers that not only had their own long histories, but also were popular with Haggar's younger target audience.

A great example of a campaign in which we utilized Haggar's partnerships to the fullest was a contest held in conjunction with the Belk Bowl, an annual college football game held in Charlotte, North Carolina, in which two VIP passes to the game were given away. Our social media team promoted the contest on Haggar's Facebook page, and also reached out to Haggar's retail partners to take advantage of their already flourishing social media audiences.

This resulted in a win-win(-win) situation—Haggar was able to access large, established Facebook audiences without having to first take the time to build up their own; the retailers were thrilled that a major manufacturer wanted to cross-promote; and an impressive number of people in just the right demographics were made aware of both Haggar and the contest.

» Your Turn

So how can you get started cross-pollinating your own marketing strategies? Here's a step-by-step guide.

1. Pick low-hanging fruit.

To start out with, assess your current marketing resources. How well are you taking advantage of your own marketing team—their strengths and areas of expertise? In order to cross-pollinate with resources outside the department effectively, you need to know what you have to begin with.

» Homes for Pets, a nonprofit focused on helping homeless pets, has a lean marketing team, but on that team they have a person with amazing photography chops, and someone else who knows how to put videos together. However, the nonprofit has them only writing blog posts and posting them on social media; in doing so, they realize, they're disregarding some of the most powerful tools for reaching an online audience: images and videos! So as an easy first step toward cross-pollination, they decide to utilize their current marketing resources more fully, by asking those team members to put together some images and videos for the organization, to add that much more momentum to their cause.

2. Use what you've learned.

Cross-pollination isn't just about your people's skills—it's about *any* resources available to you that can be tapped into for marketing purposes. Anything, including knowledge, is fair game. What have you learned from previous marketing campaigns, integrated or not? What have other, non-marketing employees at your company noticed about past marketing initiatives? Do your partners or vendors have any experience or insights to contribute? Getting multiple perspectives on past marketing campaigns is an effective way to build on prior successes and avoid past missteps.

» Homes for Pets has vast experience in running real-world adoption events. Now they begin to consider how that knowledge can be leveraged to inform online adoption events, or even just influence audience behavior in general when it comes to promoting adoption online. They tap into partner shelters and rescue groups' knowledge and experience by asking them for their input, as well.

3. Get everyone in the company on board.

Find easy ways for everyone in your company—not just the marketing team—to get involved in marketing. Every team member should be sharing your message on their personal social media accounts—make it easy for them by regularly sending them pre-written tweets and posts that can just be copied and pasted into each channel.

» Every team member at Homes for Pets is a passionate supporter of their cause, so their personal social media pages are full of posts promoting adoption, pet population control measures, fostering, and other services Homes for Pets provides. But the marketing team makes it even easier for everyone to spread the word by providing them with messages to post that correspond with in-progress campaigns and point to Homes for Pets' blog posts.

4. Find your internal subject matter experts.

In the same way that Marketade leveraged their researchers' expertise, you should locate your own company's experts and tap into their knowledge to beef up your marketing content. Whether they're informally sharing information and insights with you, which you then shape into usable content, or writing blog posts or white papers themselves, the key is to get their expertise in front of your audience.

» One member of the Homes for Pets team happens to be a veterinarian, while another worked at a shelter for years. Both of these team members have valuable contributions to offer the marketing department. Marketing asks the vet to give some in-depth medical advice and tips, and even explain the science behind various aspects of pet care, and asks the former shelter employee to give firsthand, insider accounts of what being in a shelter is like for pets. Then, they leverage these in blog posts, videos, and social media posts. Hearing something from a true expert makes the message that much more powerful to the organization's audience.

5. Check into current campaign integration.

Are your campaigns working in concert and building on each other, or are they launched separately and competing with each other, rather than with your competitors' campaigns? Is there an overall strategy that keeps the many channels you operate in working together? Cross-pollination starts with integration at home, in the marketing department.

» Homes for Pets has historically run campaigns in a pretty scattered manner, posting without a real strategy in place. They might create a hashtag on Twitter, but not reference that same campaign on Facebook . . . or write a blog post, but never share it with their social media audiences. Now, Homes for Pets is getting organized. They put a plan together to leverage the added power of integration by building multi-layer campaigns that reach across channels—blog posts shared on Facebook and Twitter, supported by additional posts on the topic on those platforms, as well as related images on Instagram and Pinterest.

6. Take a hard look at the technology you're using.

Are you keeping track of your marketing technology and making sure that it all not only works together—performing complementary roles rather than redundant (or even worse, contradictory) ones—but also works and integrates with other technology used within the company? Having your marketing technology working at cross purposes to any other technology you're using defeats the purpose of using it in the first place. If your tech is working in a marketing silo and isn't connected to the rest of the company's tech, you're not getting the benefits from your tech that you should be.

» Having such a lean marketing team, Homes for Pets has had to rely on tech solutions to help with much of its online marketing— but each of those solutions was used for just one aspect of marketing. That meant that the team had to juggle multiple software solutions—one for email, one for social media, one for content.... And you can forget about those online marketing solutions being connected to any other tech used in the company, such as donor or partner databases. The nonprofit decides to invest in a solution that not only integrates all the functions they are currently spreading out over multiple pieces of software, but also links up with the tech used by the nonprofit as a whole.

7. Look for other untapped internal resources.

Is there a non-marketing department employee who could be leveraged more strategically? Technology that is not being used to the fullest? A team member who just attended a conference on marketing to millennials who can share that information with the rest of the group? Connections that team members have with community organizations, other businesses, or industry influencers? Take every detail into consideration—the more fully you can leverage every resource, the more momentum you will build.

» Homes for Pets had a large number of willing volunteers, but those volunteers weren't being used in ways that were consistent with their strengths. It was great to have help holding adoption events at local fairs, or sharing pictures of featured shelter pets online, but the nonprofit realized they could also find out what each volunteer's expertise, experience, and connections were, and then leverage them to get the most possible momentum out of every single volunteer. They asked some volunteers to take information back to their workplaces with them to raise awareness, and others to procure donations or sponsorships from their own partners. Some volunteers were even able to get their own companies to agree to partner with the nonprofit, promoting their events and initiatives via their own digital marketing channels.

8. Assess your relationships with your strategic partners.

Now that you've scrutinized your own company, it's time to look outside, at the businesses your company is linked to. Who are your partners? If you are a B2C company, maybe it's the retailers who carry your products. If you are B2B, maybe it's the providers of the solutions you resell.

Investors, manufacturers, suppliers—don't disregard any relationship, no matter how irrelevant it may seem to marketing. You'd be surprised at what a little creativity can make out of any connection. Maybe you can involve your partners' employees in sharing your content via their own personal social media accounts. Maybe you can tap into those employees' expertise in relevant areas of your business. Maybe you can come up with creative ways to promote each other's companies in your marketing, running campaigns together. Look at every possibility.

» Homes for Pets' partners are the shelters and rescue groups they work with. They asked those organizations to promote Homes for Pets in their marketing channels, and vice versa. Employees of each began to share campaigns run by any of them. Homes for Pets started featuring different shelters, shelter employees, and different pets in their blog posts, emails, and social media.

9. Consider your connections with outside vendors.

Just as important as your strategic partner connections are your relationships with the outside vendors that provide you with goods and services. Approach these the same way you did your partners, by looking for any possible opportunity for cross-pollination, no matter how irrelevant it might seem at first glance. Even the company who provides you with office supplies or coffee could open up an entirely new direction to take with your marketing.

» Homes for Pets decides to try to leverage the company that hosts its website, the company that prints its event banners and signs, and the company that delivers the donated pet food to shelters for them. Each of these businesses, as it turns out, is more than willing to pitch in and help promote the nonprofit on their business social media pages as well as their personal ones. The printing company even runs a campaign for them on their own Facebook page—a giveaway offering a free banner to the business who comes up with the most creative Facebook post supporting Homes for Pets, boosting their own standing as community-minded, while at the same time adding momentum to the nonprofit's efforts.

10. Build new relationships as often as possible.

The more connections you create and maintain, the more possibilities will be open to you. And when those connections are made with your marketing strategy in mind, they can be even more effective at boosting your marketing momentum. Who are the influencers in your industry? Whose blogs and newsletters do you read to keep up to date in your field? Which print publications and websites do you read to stay abreast of current trends? These are the people and organizations you should create relationships with.

How can you do this? Start small, by spending some time reading the influencer's blog posts or articles and leaving comments. And just any old comment—"This is great!" or "Thanks for the interesting read!"—won't cut it here. You'll need to post well thought out, insightful comments that show the influencer that you not only read the post, but cared about the subject enough to continue the conversation.

Next, share the influencer's content with your audience on social media. Tweet links to their blog posts, for example, and mention them by their Twitter handle so they can see what you've shared. Add a comment to these social media posts as well, giving your audience a real reason to check the influencer's content out. A bump in traffic from your tweet is sure to get you into the influencer's good graces! And even if the traffic you send their way is negligible, they'll still appreciate the fact that you found their content valuable enough to share.

Finally, introduce yourself. Once you're already a somewhat familiar figure from their blog comments section and social media, send a friendly email introducing yourself and letting them know how much you like their work. By formalizing the connection with an email introduction, you'll be solidifying your relationship, and opening the channels of communication.

» Homes for Pets realized that local animal welfare bloggers and even pet stores would be the most effective influencers to develop relationships with. They began to cultivate connections with local pet stores, both boutique and chain, as well as with bloggers with large online audiences who are passionate about the cause, by commenting on the stores' and bloggers' blog posts and social media posts, sharing the links with their own followers, and then finally, emailing to initiate a real relationship with each.

11. Leverage those new relationships.

Your ultimate goal with most influencers will be to get them to agree to let you guest post on their site, which allows you the opportunity to share your message with a brand new audience in your own voice—although you could also ask if they would like to partner to promote your company on their website in other ways, such as reviewing your product themselves or linking to your website in a post. But before you approach them, make sure you fully understand which kinds of topics the influencer focuses on, and what their audience expects. If you approach an influencer asking to write a guest post that doesn't make sense for their site, you'll be instantly damaging your credibility—and your relationship.

Email the influencer to suggest a relevant topic you might write about, and explain how your particular brand of expertise would benefit their audience. While your aim in guest blogging is to raise awareness of your business within the influencer's audience, the influencer doesn't care about that. What they want is a post that will be of real value to their audience—and bolster their own reputation. Be the person who gives them an easy way to do just that.

If you've done your relationship-building homework well, your chosen blogger just might agree to partner with you. You'll be able to reach an entirely new audience with your message, showcasing your expertise to a slew of potential new customers and drawing them to your own site with a link in your bio or in the post itself. But more importantly, you'll have created a mutually beneficial relationship with your new friend—one that could bear fruit for years to come.

» In order to leverage their newfound relationships with influencers, Homes for Pets began a campaign to guest blog on their sites—and asked influencers to guest blog on their own site as well. This helped both parties expand their reach, while strengthening the relationship on both sides.

12. Close the loop.

Finally, why not continue the cross-pollination and integration by introducing some of your connections to each other? If your relationship with a vendor allows you to make life easier for a partner by connecting the two with each other, why wouldn't you take that extra step and create even more goodwill on all sides? And if you prove yourself to be a valuable connection to have, the right people will be lining up to work with you—which in turn gives you even more options for cross-pollination.

》 With all of its connections across industries, Homes for Pets is able to connect their business partners with other partners who need their services, other animal-related nonprofits with businesses that can help support them, and animal lovers with like-minded people passionate about homeless pets and willing to do what it takes to help. All that mutual support leads to everyone feeling more fulfilled.

》 Cross-Pollination Tools

It's one thing to cross-pollinate; it's another to keep track of all the various moving parts of such a complex endeavor. There aren't yet many tools available to make this seamless, but more are being created every day.

One valuable software tool currently on the market is Bionic Marketing Performance Management, which tracks many aspects of your integrated marketing strategy, from vendor costs to online marketing metrics. It does this not by aggregating data from all your various online marketing channels, but by aggregating data from all your various marketing automation platforms. Online and offline activities are connected and tracked. Each individual campaign's performance can be easily observed.

Cross-pollination means leveraging and integrating every single resource available to you, and having such a meta overview of every aspect of your business, but with the ability to drill down into the details, gives you the tools you need to keep up with it all as well as look for new opportunities.

» Cross-Pollination Tips

Especially when you're just getting started with cross-pollination, the best plan is to start slowly, integrating just a few elements at a time, until you build up to full cross-pollination. One of the easiest places to begin is integrating your email and social media marketing efforts.

Email marketing is one of a marketer's most effective ways of driving conversions. Polls have shown again and again that customers prefer to receive sales messages via email, as opposed to any other medium, and studies have proven that email drives sales.

Social media marketing is one of the very best ways for your brand to connect with an online audience—you can use it to create communities, nurture relationships, and build a strong network of brand ambassadors who will provide online word-of-mouth advertising for your business.

Each of these on its own is a powerful marketing tool. So, can you imagine the results you'd produce, and the momentum you'd be harnessing, by integrating even just these two marketing channels?

Of course integration doesn't mean simply using both email and social media in your marketing strategy. True integration—cross-pollination—means syncing the two marketing channels as closely as possible, using each to link to the other and creating a seamless experience for customers that provides all the benefits of both marketing channels—while boosting the power of each exponentially.

Don't think of these marketing methods as separate entities. Instead, think of them as two sides of the same coin. Each side should be inextricably connected to the other. Here are some tips to help get you started strategizing:

1. Add social media icons to emails.

First, the obvious: Every single email you send should include social media icons. This is the easiest and most common way to link your email marketing activities with your social media marketing efforts—and the reason it's so common is that it works. Every email subscriber on your list should be reminded of all your social media channels each time they get a message from you, and should be provided with a convenient way to connect with you on each of them.

2. Add social media share buttons, as well.

This is another no-brainer. In addition to encouraging your email recipients to connect with you on social media, you should also be prompting them to share your emails with their own personal social media networks.

3. Coordinate email subject lines and Facebook headlines.

For the most part, your audience on Facebook and your email list have similar interests and preferences, and may even consist of many of the same people. So what works well on one platform will likely work well on the other. If you've found success using a particular email subject line, try the same approach in a Facebook headline—and if you've gotten a lot of engagement from a particular Facebook headline, use it as an email subject line.

4. Incorporate video into your emails.

Video is the latest addition to the email marketing world, and one that can make a dramatic difference in conversions. Now that more email providers have enabled videos, actually sending out videos you've posted to YouTube—social media's video hub—can work as a powerful tool for getting attention and encouraging clicks. For recipients who can't view the video in their email, be sure to include a link to the video, as well.

5. Include social media fan interactions in your emails.

Think of your emails as a channel for broadcasting what happens on social media—and of your social media posts as channels for broadcasting what your emails are about. Send out emails that highlight the best comments, fan images, and conversations happening on your social media networks—not only will it make for interesting content, but it will also make people want to get in on the fun themselves.

6. Feature a social media fan of the month in your emails.

Focusing in on one particular fan can be another great way to drive engagement. That fan will share the email with his network, and others will be motivated to interact with your brand via social media in order to be chosen themselves.

7. Announce upcoming emails on social media.

In keeping with tip #5, use social media as a place to spread the word about the content in your emails. To make people want to subscribe, give them tantalizing sneak peeks at what they're missing out on.

8. Share links to web-based versions of your emails on social media.

Once an email has gone out, leverage it even further by letting your social media fans see its content, too. If they like what they see, they'll probably subscribe so they won't risk missing one in the future.

9. Use your interactions with fans on Facebook to determine email content.

Observe what the most popular topics are on your Facebook page, or come right out and ask fans what they'd like to see in your emails. Not only will your emails be tailored more specifically to your customers' interests, but Facebook fans who aren't already will want to sign up to receive the content they had a hand in asking for.

10. Ask for the conversion.

In your emails, ask recipients to like your Facebook page. And on your Facebook page, ask fans to opt-in to your email list. The more points of contact you have with your audience, the better. In fact, you could even send an email dedicated solely to asking recipients to connect with your brand on a certain social media platform. Maybe it's an email telling them about the benefits of following you on Twitter, or one about how much fun they could have if they joined you on Pinterest. If you are trying to grow your community on any or all social media platforms, invite your subscribers first!

11. Allow people to subscribe to your emails using their social media logins.

That way, when someone new comes across your website, you'll be able to capture both their email address and their social media information at once.

12. Send emails spreading the word about your Facebook store.

If you've dived wholeheartedly into the world of Facebook commerce, or F-commerce, you'll want to share that information with your email subscribers. Send them pictures and descriptions of the products you offer through Facebook to encourage them to visit.

A COMPANY GETTING IT RIGHT

One Marketing Zen client achieved strong cross-polli-nation momentum through an internal newsletter. Of course, email newsletters sent out to clients and prospects are a vital part of online marketing, but an internal email newsletter aimed at employees and strategic partners is another targeted way to integrate all resources available to you in order to maximize your digital marketing ROI.

As an investment bank, our client needed to demonstrate their expertise and industry thought leadership to their online audience by sharing high-quality, educational content on a regular basis. One or two employees sharing content would have been a solid marketing activity, but we wanted to really knock it out of the park—so we asked every single employee, in multiple offices spread across the country, to share their company's blog posts, PR hits, and articles with their own networks via Twitter, LinkedIn, and any other social media platforms they used.

We knew that most investment bankers would not con-sistently have time to find new content to share, and then create tweets and posts for each different social media site. So we made it easy for them. Every week, we sent out an internal newsletter chock full of relevant, timely, and educational blog posts and articles for employees to share—but we didn't stop there.

We shortened the URLs for them and created easily shareable tweets, ready-to-go LinkedIn posts, and other pre-written social media posts with hashtags and mentions and all, so that it was simply a matter of copying and pasting. We even set up Buffer accounts for each employee, so that they didn't even need to go to each social media site to post at various times throughout the week—instead, all they had to do was schedule each post from within Buffer, and voilà! Done—and it would look to their followers as if they were busily posting throughout the week.

Employee buy-in was incredibly high, and in the very first month, traffic to the client's site increased by a whopping 33 percent. The resulting marketing momentum was unbelievable. And all because the client was willing to integrate every resource available to them.

13. Let email subscribers know about social media contests.

If you are holding a contest or giveaway on social media, don't keep it a secret! Send an email to let your subscribers know what they're missing out on if they don't connect with you via social media.

14. Post links on social media to registration-required content.

Promoting a new e-book or white paper, or even a webinar or podcast? Let your social media networks know about it—but only allow access if they sign up to receive your emails, too.

15. Use social media to boost the momentum of any email marketing campaigns you run.

Don't stop at just sending an email—ask recipients a campaign-related question in your email that they are directed to answer on Facebook. Or ask them to post pictures or videos to your social media pages. If you're running a Valentine's Day email campaign, ask customers to upload images that show just how much they love your product to a Pinterest board or tag them with the right hashtag on Instagram, for example. Keep that momentum going for as long as you can by encouraging social media engagement.

Marketers today do best when they take a lesson from bees, mixing and matching "marketing pollen" to infuse their strategies with new power. By utilizing and integrating every last resource available to you, whether internal or external, human or tech, as additional tools in your digital marketing strategy, you can create campaigns that far outpace a siloed approach to marketing.

Chapter 6 Takeaways

» Cross-pollination means integrating every single resource your company has into your marketing strategy, allowing each to inform your use of the others.

» Integration of current campaigns and related tech elements is vital for cross-pollination.

» Cross-pollination is all about connections and relationships.

» A good place to start your cross-pollination efforts is by integrating your email and social media marketing.

chapter **7**

Measuring Marketing ROI in the Digital Age

GILITY. CUSTOMER FOCUS. Integration. Content curation. Cross-pollination. These are the five principles that
drive marketing momentum today.

Agility drives momentum by allowing companies to strategically fan the flames of their marketing successes—to change
tack instantly when analytics show them where to focus.

Customer focus drives momentum by tapping into the
human desire to project a certain image of ourselves, and by
harnessing your audience's eagerness to engage with campaigns
tailored to their preferences and centered around them.

Integration drives momentum by enabling digital and traditional marketing to build on each other's successes.

Content curation drives momentum by providing customers with valuable information, given context by a company's
unique filter, and organized in such a way that website visitors
feel they are being guided though the content by an experienced
hand.

Cross-pollination drives momentum by integrating every single resource your company has into your marketing strategy, allowing each to inform your use of the others, so that something new and powerful is created from the synergy.

If you've followed my step-by-step instructions in each chapter, then you're well on your way to embracing the new digital marketing mindset. You're using analytics to be more agile; you're focusing campaigns on your customers; you're going digical; you're curating content the right way; and you're using every resource you have to inform and supercharge your marketing efforts. With the momentum building, and work ongoing every day to boost it even further, you're sure to start seeing some great things happening.

But there's one more aspect of marketing in the digital age that we haven't discussed yet. The world of business is all about the bottom line, and if an investment of time, effort, and money isn't paying off with a respectable ROI, it will get nixed—or at the very least, relegated to the bottom of the priority list. And far too often, marketers have a hard time demonstrating ROI in the digital age. Sure, they have plenty of data about website visits and email opens and social media likes, but when it comes to showing how those various metrics actually make their company money, they're at a loss.

If they can't prove to their boss that their work is actually making the company money, then all the marketing momentum in the world won't mean a thing.

That's why this chapter focuses on what is perhaps the most important aspect of today's marketing ecosystem: measuring marketing ROI.

There's an old adage that goes, "We know that 50 percent of our marketing is working—we just don't know which 50 percent!" These days, marketers have much more data available to them than ever before about every aspect of their marketing— and yet, it's still extremely difficult to pinpoint the exact customer journey that leads to a sale.

» Why Tracking ROI in the Digital Age Is Difficult

Years ago, the customer's journey was much more straightforward. He saw a billboard, called the phone number, and ordered the service. She saw a TV commercial, went to the store, and bought the item. The marketing principle of seven "touches" applied—the concept that a customer needs to come in contact with a brand at least seven times before he or she feels comfortable buying from them. Those touches were most likely repeated commercials, or a combination of print ads, commercials, and in-store sightings. The customer's journey was fairly straightforward, and the last point of contact was often considered the impetus for the sale.

Nowadays, customers' journeys vary wildly. One customer may see a TV commercial, go online to visit the company's website, sign up for their email newsletter, check out what some review sites have to say about them, and then buy. Another may see an online ad, click through to a landing page for a free download, then hop over to the company's Facebook page before deciding to buy. And unlike before, when the last point of contact was the impetus for the sale, today, each point of contact is cumulative and builds on the previous ones, so that the customer gathers momentum himself as he progresses.

If that first customer had never done his research on the company's website, he would never have checked out those review sites and ultimately been persuaded to buy—and yet, the website analytics will show that he came, looked around for a bit, and left without buying. If that second customer had never seen the online ad, she would never have even known about the company—but since she came directly from Facebook to buy, the social media platform gets all the credit. The metrics that marketers usually track are valuable, but they don't give us a very good picture of this new multi-touch, multi-point customer journey.

Measuring ROI used to be a linear matter. Now, it's much more complex. When consumers were marketed *to*—were passive recipients of marketing—it was easy to draw those lines from contact to sale. With customers taking initiative and seeking out marketing themselves, their motivations are not as easy to track. In spite of that, most companies still cling to the old ways of determining ROI—and come away disappointed in their marketing because of it.

» What ROI Means in the Digital Age

Before we can start measuring ROI, it's important to understand what ROI means today. The old concept of ROI as a purely numbers-based metric is no longer valid. Yes, quantitative measurements are vital, but they're not the only ones that are important. Qualitative measurements are just as important—and can actually be measured in numbers these days as well, through software that scans social media, blogs, and other sites for mentions of your brand and then determines the balance of positive versus negative comments. When customer sentiment towards your brand is mostly positive, you can rest assured that you're getting your marketing right, even if the metric doesn't fit into traditional ideas of ROI.

There are also many non-linear, non-sales-related benefits of marketing that just don't show up on the radar unless you know to look for them. For example, social media allows a company to get instant feedback on new product ideas, minimizing the need to spend millions on focus groups or research and development. That's a perk that wouldn't necessarily come up in a standard assessment of ROI, but with that kind of money at stake, it definitely should.

So what does marketing ROI mean in the digital age? It means looking for ROI in non-traditional places, and counting qualitative measurements just as much as quantitative ones.

» Why Aren't You Getting Marketing ROI?

Another step before you start measuring your marketing ROI is to be sure you have marketing ROI to measure! If you've been doing everything you can think of to increase your marketing ROI, but haven't met with much success, you may be tempted to throw in the towel and complain that marketing simply doesn't produce a real ROI. Nothing could be further from the truth. If you're not seeing any return from your hard work, ask yourself the following questions:

1. Is your marketing truly integrated?

Remember our talk about integration in chapter 4? How about our discussion of cross-pollination in chapter 6? Integration is a major component of today's marketing paradigm, and without it, you simply can't expect success on a high level. Integrating your marketing and cross-pollinating all of your company's resources are what allow you to build momentum, and that momentum is what leads to ROI.

2. Is your marketing consistent in its execution?

It's all well and good to have the perfect strategy in place, but if your execution is lacking, it won't do you any good. Blog posts have to be published regularly. Social media posts should be on a schedule. Emails need to go out on a regular basis. When people sign up for emails but only receive them sporadically, or visit a Facebook page only to see that posts are few and far between, they come away with a negative view of your company. Why would anyone spend money with a company that can't even get its act together enough to put an email together once a week? Consistency is key to building consumer trust, and that trust is what will compel them to buy—giving you your ROI.

3. Do you have "Oh, look, a squirrel!" syndrome?

Do you immediately jump on the bandwagon of every new marketing trend that bursts onto the scene? While some new platforms end up having staying power, others gradually fade from the limelight and then disappear quietly—and anyone who invested time and money into marketing through the latter is out of luck. Waiting a little while to see how things pan out is a good way to avoid losing time and energy invested in a failed enterprise.

Another version of this problem is the marketer who is constantly jumping to new marketing tools, whether software, online platforms, or even new strategies—and then neglecting to follow through with the necessary work to use them properly. The thrill of exploring a new avenue begins to fade, and then—oh, look, a squirrel! And he's off and running again.

ROI isn't produced overnight. It takes time and effort. Jumping from one platform to the next without giving any of them a chance to work guarantees that none of them will.

4. Are you too focused on linear ROI?

As I mentioned, marketing ROI is a different animal today than it was even just a few years ago. Insisting on treating today's marketing methods as if they were no different from traditional marketing methods is bound to end in failure. We're not comparing apples to apples here—it's more like apples to Ford Model T cars. The production of one is simple and straightforward, and can be measured in the same way, while the other requires an entire assembly line of actions and moving parts, all of which must be taken into consideration to result in a meaningful measurement.

5. Is there a problem with your product or service?

If all else fails, it may be that your product or service itself needs tweaking or even a complete overhaul. The best marketing in the world won't produce ROI for a product that people just don't want. Take a good look at your audience's feedback online to see what they think—and by doing so, you'll have gotten yourself some ROI already!

» Defining the R in ROI

So now that you understand your current ROI situation, let's take a look at what measurements to look at in determining that all-important metric.

Basically, it all boils down to this: what you measure depends completely on your goals.

Begin with the end in mind. What are you trying to do with this campaign? The answer to that question will inform what metrics you track.

- If you're looking to improve your revenue online, you'll be focused on traffic, leads, and reach.
- If you want to boost traffic to your company website, you'll be looking at analytics from your website, blog, social networks, and search engines.
- If you are trying to diversify your traffic sources, you'll be considering direct traffic, organic search, referrals, email, and PPC.
- And if you are looking to boost on-site conversions, you'll look at lead generation, click-throughs, and landing page copy.

» How to Measure Marketing ROI

Just as different metrics matter for different goals, different marketing channels require different methods of measurement.

Email Marketing

Any email marketing platform you use will give you data about a significant number of metrics, from opens to clicks to landing page conversions, but some go more in-depth than others, and can actually calculate the value of each subscriber and each conversion based on sales data. Using these metrics, you can easily measure the ROI of your list-building and email marketing efforts by assessing the value of all subscribers.

PPC Advertising

PPC, or pay-per-click, advertising may be the easiest form of marketing to measure ROI for, due to the incredible amount of data available about every aspect of your ads and the way customers engage with them: the number of impressions (pageviews), the number of click-throughs, the popularity of the keywords you use, and more. In order to use this data to measure PPC ROI, try using dedicated landing pages for your ads. By tracking the visits to these pages, you'll find out exactly how valuable the traffic you're paying for is: how much of it is converting, what level of revenue it's bringing in. Then, you can calculate the cost of acquiring your leads, the ROI from each of those leads, and your overall PPC ROI as well.

SEO

Measuring the ROI on search engine optimization may not be as easy as it is with email marketing or PPC, but by putting in just a little bit of effort in the beginning, you can set up a valuable method of measurement.

First, before performing the optimization, measure your historic website traffic, conversions, and revenue levels, in order to come up with a baseline.

Next, decide what your conversion goals are for your marketing efforts. It may be something as straightforward as sales or something more to do with engagement and building an audience, like adding subscribers to your newsletter.

Then, set up a Google Analytics Goal that tracks conversion rates for traffic coming in from organic search (i.e., the traffic captured by your SEO). You can then determine the cost of acquiring a customer by comparing the amount of money you spend on SEO services to the amount of money a conversion from organic traffic is worth.

Website Improvements

It's also possible to measure the ROI from updating and redesigning your website, whether that involves a complete overhaul of the content and design, slight tweaking of certain pages, or a switch to responsive, mobile-friendly design. To measure ROI, track your number of website visitors, your click-through rates from dedicated landing pages, your conversion rates—whether for online sales, email newsletter signups, completed online forms, white paper downloads, or some other action—and any increase in revenue generated via the site. Then compare to previous numbers to ascertain ROI.

Social Media Marketing

While measuring ROI for these other marketing efforts is pretty straightforward, calculating social media marketing ROI can be more challenging. Engagement, audience reach, buzz, and customer sentiment can't be measured directly. Luckily, they can be ascertained through metrics like the number of fans, followers, page likes, retweets, repins, and web mentions. In addition to these metrics, here are ten more ways to measure social media marketing ROI:

- **Sales:** Your bottom line is one of your biggest indicators that your social media is working. In this era of multi-touch marketing, your sales shouldn't be forgotten. But remember, social media ROI isn't visible instantaneously. One of my favorite quotes about being patient when waiting for ROI comes from Jeff Bezos, founder and CEO of Amazon. He said: "I always tell people, if we have a good quarter it's because of the work we did three, four, and five years ago. It's not because we did a good job this quarter." This is the *key* to social media marketing success.
- **Closing ratio:** If people trust your company, chances are that they will move forward with you much more often than not. They will choose you over your competitors. A higher closing ratio tells you your marketing—not just your sales process—is working.
- **Length of sales cycle:** Especially in the B2B world, the bigger the purchase, the longer the sales cycle. A big part of the sales cycle is educating the prospect. Your social media

should contribute to this education, making the prospect's decision easier—and the sales cycle shorter.

- **Leads:** This is perhaps the most obvious one. Are you getting more leads? Be sure to have a phone number and contact form easily accessible on your social media pages as well as your website.

- **New visitors:** Are you attracting new people to your website? Your social media marketing should not only be strengthening relationships with existing customers, but also, ideally, attracting an audience you weren't previously engaging.

- **Brand perception:** What are people saying about you, your brand, your industry on social media? How you are perceived can truly dictate your success.

- **Bounce rate:** This is what I call the "sticky factor" (much to our SEO department's chagrin). Your bounce rate can be found using Google Analytics, and tells you how many initial visitors, upon arrival on your website, hit the back button or went to a different website instead of delving deeper into yours. When visitors have already had an introduction to you via social media and feel you and your site are trustworthy, chances are they will stick around, and your bounce rate will be lower. A low bounce rate also signifies a higher quality of visitor: Someone who is truly interested in what you have to offer is more likely to browse your content for a longer period of time.

- **Social media platform metrics:** This is what most people measure to gauge their social media success, and there is a lot of controversy here. Is the key to social media momentum quantity or quality? Both, actually. High quantities of quality Twitter followers, Facebook fans, and LinkedIn connections—meaning those who are actively engaged with your content—are all viable metrics of your social media marketing success.

- **Newsletter and blog subscribers:** There are two types of conversions that happen online. The first is what people are familiar with—direct conversion of website visitors to customers or clients. The second type of conversion is less well-known, but perhaps even more crucial. It is when a website visitor turns into a consumer. They choose to consume your information—which is the first step towards becoming a customer or a client. Measuring your consumers (blog subscribers, for example) is an excellent way to determine social media ROI.

- **PR:** Reporters like companies and individuals who are smart, authentic, and strike a chord with the public. Social media makes it easy for reporters to find you. It makes it easier for you to showcase your company culture and personal brand. It allows you to build relationships with bloggers. And creating a buzz on social media and online attracts reporters looking for a potentially popular story. More PR requests can be a great indicator that your social media marketing is making a real impact.

» ROI Measurement in Action

Let's return one last time to our friends at Marketade, and see how they approach the issue of measuring marketing ROI.

For each of the campaigns Stan and Savanna put in place, goals were determined beforehand. In the case of the free drink offer, Marketade's goal was to persuade as many people as possible to redeem the offer, in order to boost sales, brand awareness, and customer sentiment.

The redemption of the offer was easy to track—Marketade knew exactly who was picking up their free drinks, and who wasn't, due to unique codes in the coupon. But how did the offer redemption affect sales, and especially intangibles like brand awareness and customer sentiment?

Because there are two types of ROI here—quantitative and qualitative—Marketade measured it in two different ways. First, quantitative. Baselines of historic sales were determined to compare new sales against. The numbers would be compared to sales from the same time the previous year, as well as sales performance immediately prior to the beginning of the campaign. Then, those revenues would be measured against the amount spent on the campaign. Pretty straightforward, right?

The qualitative aspect was not quite so simple to track—but with today's tools, could be determined nonetheless. Here's how they did it.

Social listening software was used to find mentions of Marketade across the web—on social media, in blogs, on review sites, and anywhere else customers might be discussing the brand. The software provided an overview of whether customer sentiment was more positive or more negative, and also gave Stan and Savanna an idea of how brand awareness was spreading, based on how many mentions were found and which channels they were in.

Marketade also looked at social media metrics such as likes, new fans and followers, and clicks. These numbers may not say much when it comes to sales, but when it comes to customer sentiment, they provide a useful way to track growth. Stan and Savanna also checked the number of new visitors to the Marketade site, in order to track growth of brand awareness. Finally, they looked into the number of PR requests they had received since the start of the campaign, and compared that to the pre-campaign number.

Stan and Savanna found that as far as sales went, they had a respectable ROI from their marketing efforts. All the work that had gone into boosting the momentum of their campaign, from using analytics to make changes that took advantage of the momentum already building, to customizing their tactics to fit their customer personas, had paid off in terms of increased sales.

They found, too, that those sales were driven by an accompanying increase in brand awareness and customer sentiment. Because Marketade made it easy, fun, and appealing for their target audience to share the offer with their friends, the Marketade name—and the positive image of the company that customers so enjoyed associating themselves with—spread like wildfire among online communities of like-minded friends.

Savanna and Stan know that today's marketing is multi-touch, and that attributing the ROI to one point of contact in the marketing process would not only be wrong, it would discount the very real part that other elements played in moving customers along the sales funnel. Without the qualitative, there would be very little quantitative.

Executives at Marketade also understood this, and so they were more than satisfied with the results and the ROI of their campaign. They continue to follow the five principles of momentum in order to get their campaigns to snowball into huge successes. And they continue to monitor their results and their ROI to ensure that what they are doing in marketing is matching up with their overall business goals.

⟫ COMPANIES GETTING IT RIGHT

Here are some examples of companies successfully tracking ROI from multi-touch marketing campaigns:

- Starbucks once ran a commercial during *Saturday Night Live*, as well as on YouTube, advertising a free coffee giveaway. Mentions of Starbucks on Twitter skyrocketed, with an average of one mention every eight seconds! Tracking this metric allowed Starbucks to see how brand awareness had been affected by their campaign.
- When Naked Pizza, a New Orleans-based business whose customer base is composed of health-conscious pizza lovers, first started tweeting about its pizzas, it managed to attract about 4,000 followers in just a few months. The company also bought a billboard that encouraged customers to follow Naked Pizza on Twitter. The campaign ended up helping the company break its one-day sales record, with more than 68 percent of its sales coming

---

from customers who said they were Twitter followers. When polled, incredibly, 85 percent of the new customers said they had made the decision to buy from Naked Pizza because of Twitter. ROI on steroids!

- Target came up with a campaign to leverage the social networking aspect of Facebook for its marketing purposes by encouraging customers to join and participate in an online community for moms that was set up by Target but did not include any promotional messaging. Target tracked the results of its campaign by watching the number of membership sign-ups. Thousands ended up joining, and generating significant buzz with their enthusiastic participation, which in turn prompted many others to join and participate, as well. A connected Facebook application called Circle of Moms—which let mothers post messages, arrange carpools, set up back-to-school checklists, and click through to promotions on the Target site—attracted more than 20,000 users in six weeks. This campaign built goodwill and further positive brand awareness for Target—resulting in higher sales.

- The Japanese gaming company Square Enix started its own online community to create interest in its North American release of Sony's PlayStation 2 video game *Dragon Quest VIII: Journey of the Cursed King*. The effort was a huge success, attracting more than 14,000 members, with 30 percent of them reporting having been recruited via word of mouth from existing members. According to polls, 40 percent of the online community pre-ordered the game. By the end of its first year the video game had sold 510,000 units in North America.

- Burger King once created a Facebook app called Whopper Sacrifice, which asked users to unfriend ten of their Facebook friends in exchange for a free Whopper. The application monitored who had been unfriended, and sent those users alerts informing them that they had been sacrificed for a Whopper, and inviting them to do the same with their friends list—which continued to build momentum for the campaign. In the end, the campaign resulted in users unfriending a total of 234,000 Facebook friends.

» Make Your Own Momentum

So here we are—at the end and also at the beginning of the cycle that defines marketing in the digital age. Data and analytics are the starting point for any good campaign, and in the end, they show you just how successful that campaign was.

Measuring ROI, though difficult in this multi-touch world, is vital for the future success of any business. Accumulating the numbers that tell the story of how effective your campaign was allows you to tweak your strategy based on performance. Those same numbers tell you how well you knew your customers and tailored your campaign to their preferences—as well as how strategically you were able to integrate digital and traditional marketing activities. Your ROI will also let you know how effective your content curation strategy was, and will show you how fully you were able to leverage all the resources available to you.

Armed with this information, you can dive into your next campaign with the assurance of even greater momentum the next time around.

acknowledgments

It really does take a village . . .

My sincerest and deepest gratitude to all those who have
made this book a reality.

To all my readers: I thank you! There is no greater gift for an
author than an engaged reader.

To my amazing team at The Marketing Zen Group: You
inspire me with your passion and your excellence.

To all our clients: Your continued trust and support is what
makes everything possible. From the bottom of my heart,
thank you.

To Angela von Weber-Hahnsberg: Your hard work made this
book a reality.

To David Kirkpatrick: Thank you for all your research.

To Janet Goldstein and Elizabeth Marshall, for inspiring me, believing in me, and cheering me on every step of the way.

To the entire team at BenBella Books—including my inimitable editor, Leah Wilson—without whom this book would not have been possible.

index

about the author

Called the "Zen Master of Marketing" by *Entrepreneur* magazine and the "Millennial Master of the Universe" by *Fast Company*, Shama Hyder is a visionary strategist for the digital age.

She is the bestselling author of *The Zen of Social Media Marketing* and an acclaimed international keynote speaker who's been invited to share the stage with the world's top leaders, including President Obama and the Dalai Lama.

As the founder and CEO, she's led the award-winning integrated online marketing and digital PR firm Marketing Zen Group to become a global industry leader. Her company has been honored by both the White House and the United Nations as one of the top 100 U.S. companies run by a young entrepreneur, as curated by Empact100.

A trusted media expert and sought-after TV personality, Shama is a frequent contributor on Fox, Bloomberg, CNBC, MSNBC, and more. As a thought leader, she's been featured in many major publications, including *The New York Times*, *The Wall Street Journal*, *Entrepreneur*, *Inc.* magazine, and *Forbes*.

Shama has been listed as a 25 Under 25 entrepreneur by *BusinessWeek* and a 30 Under 30 entrepreneur by *Inc.* magazine. She was recently named to the 2015 *Forbes'* 30 Under 30 list of movers and shakers.

For information on booking Shama for a keynote or serve as a brand ambassador, or for media queries, please visit:

www.ShamaHyder.com

want to accelerate your momentum?

Don't just read about it. Put it into action!

Learn how to apply the Five Principles of *Momentum* to your business or organization with a FREE interactive e-course—developed exclusively for readers of this book.

With the e-course, you'll get a clear picture of how to integrate all five principles into your overall marketing plan and identify immediate ways to boost the overall ROI of your marketing efforts.

This free companion course to the book includes:

- » Video lessons
- » Cheat sheets
- » Infographics
- » Case studies
- » Tools and resources

For immediate and free access to your free e-course, sign up now at:

momentum.pub

a freshly updated, expanded, and newly revised edition of the ultimate primer and how-to guide for social media marketing

"Highly recommended for anybody with anything to market online—including him or herself."

—from *Library Journal*

Five years ago, the first edition of *The Zen of Social Media Marketing* became a global bestseller. Three years after that, the updated edition helped even more marketers and executives navigate the sometimes-stressful world of social media. Now, this new, up-to-date edition offers timely insight to the ways social media has changed and how best to market in it.

With a foreword by *New York Times* bestselling author Chris Brogan and new and updated content on content marketing, email marketing, the importance of mobile, social advertising, and more, the newest edition of *The Zen of Social Media Marketing* gives you:

- A comprehensive overview of why social media works and how to use it to drive traffic to your website and fan page
- A proven process to attract followers and fans and convert them into customers and clients
- The latest social media trends and step-by-step guidelines for sites and apps such as Instagram, Pinterest, Snapchat, Imgur, LINE, and more
- All new information on why, when, and how to use online advertising
- Innovative tips for mobile design
- Essential advice on content marketing and targeted tactics to enhance your SEO
- Why self-expression is the true driver of social media use and how to leverage it for your business
- Insights from dozens of leading online marketers and entrepreneurs, with strategies for success

shamahyder.com